A History of Lifelong Learning
at Cardiff University
1883–2008

Marian Williams

First published in 2008 by

Cardiff Centre for Lifelong Learning
Senghennydd Road,
Cardiff
CF24 4AG
tel +44 02920 870000
fax +44 02920 668935
learn@cardiff.ac.uk
www.cardiff.ac.uk/learn

We gratefully acknowledge support from 'Cardiff 125' toward
the cost of this publication.

ISBN 978-0-9561156-0-7

cover and book design by Ian Spring
printed by A McLay & Co. Ltd

Contents

Acknowledgements

I am grateful to a number of people who helped me in the production of this work. My thanks to Sara Phillips, Cardiff University Records & Institutional Archives Officer, Corporate Compliance Unit, for providing me with many primary sources from the University Archives and to Michael Wilcox of the Glamorgan Record Office who made available to me documents in connection with the University Settlement. Thanks too to Peter Keelan and his staff at SCOLAR in the Arts and Social Studies Library for general help in locating University Calendars, photographs, etc and for providing me with a quiet place in which to work. The contributions of Gwen Awbery, Gill Boden, Royston Havard, John Pikoulis, Peter Webster and Jan Stephens are, of course, very much appreciated. And last but not least, thanks to Richard Evans and David Wyatt for suggesting and initiating the project and to Ian Spring for editing and designing this book.

Foreword

Due to circumstances beyond my control, I was denied the opportunity of a university education. However, at the age of sixty, when perhaps I should have been contemplating retirement, I applied for, and was offered a place at Cardiff University to read history and so began for me ten years, first as an undergraduate and then as a postgraduate student that were among the happiest and most fulfilling of my life.

It all began at the Cardiff Centre for Lifelong Learning (as it is now called) in the early 1990s. As an employee of the University, I worked in a building just opposite the offices of the Centre, then in Park Place in the old BBC building, so it made sense to take advantage of some of the lunchtime University courses that were on offer. The fees were reasonable and so at various times I attended classes in literature, poetry and art and, more recently, law and criminology and enjoyed them all. However, the series of lectures that changed my life were those on history. I chose to attend the lectures on American presidents that were given by Dr Graham Watson and found them so stimulating that by the time the course finished I knew that I wanted more and was driven to do something about it. I finally had the confidence to apply for a full-time place at Cardiff and, as the saying goes, the rest is history.

For contextual reasons, this short history of lifelong learning in Cardiff will begin with an overview of adult education facilities in the Principality prior to the establishment, in 1883, of the new University in Cardiff. As intimated in the University's founding Charter of 1884, community engagement, adult education and what we now term 'widening access' were, and remain, an integral part of the University's mission.

The development of the University's lifelong learning programme is charted from the late nineteenth century until the present day; through the peaks and troughs of provision, through periods of social unrest, recession, and global conflict, and the shifting tides of government legislation. Moreover, the University's changing initiatives and the financial, staffing and logistical difficulties which it faced as it attempted to develop lifelong learning and raise the aspirations of the local community more generally are investigated and assessed.

Marian Williams, 2008

Illustrations (between pages 44 and 45)

1. The old infirmary building in Newport Road which was the original home of the University College of South Wales and Monmouthshire, 1883.
2. The old infirmary building, 1933.
3. Temporary science laboratories in Newport Road.
4. Temporary science laboratories in Newport Road.
5. Professor A G Little, Professor of History 1892-1901.
6. The University's Royal Charter.
7. Prospectus for extension lectures 1901-1902.
8. Ronald Burrows, Professor of Greek at Cardiff 1897-1908.
9. The University Settlement buildings in Walker Road and Courtenay Road.
10. Viriamu Jones, Principal 1883-1901.
11. A H Trow, Principal 1918-1929.
12. Ivor James, Registrar 1883-1895.
13. D J A Brown, Registrar 1913-c1933.
14. A F Dixon, Professor of Anatomy 1897-1902.
15. Cardiff Centre for Lifelong Learning 2008.

Items 1, 2, 10, 11, 12 & 13 are reproduced from *A Short History of the College 1883-1933* by A H Trow & D J A Brown. Items 3 & 4 are reproduced from *University College Cardiff, a centenary history* by S B Chrimes. Item 8 is reproduced from *Ronald Burrows, a memoir* by G Glasgow. Item 9 can be found at http://www.geograph.org.uk/photo/121519 and is credited to Linda Bailey. Item 14 was provided by Professor Bernard Moxham, Deputy Director and Head of Teaching, Cardiff School of Biosciences and reproduced by Robert Jones, Cardiff School of Biosciences. We are grateful for permission to reproduce these illustrations.

Lifelong learning in South Wales: a historical background

Adult education and urban growth were closely linked in the rapidly industrialising society that was nineteenth-century Britain. Although the term 'urban growth' evokes instant images of geographical expansion, probably its most important component is the human one – the people who generate the ideas, the investment and the labour that fuels and directs industry and commerce towards economic success. In order to keep pace with, or better still to forge ahead of, rival economies, the intellectual as well as the physical well-being of a nation is of prime importance.[1] This fact was recognised long before a university was established in Cardiff and it is worth taking a brief glance at the earlier history of education, mainly directed at children but eventually expanded to embrace adults too.

It is well known that from the earliest times the church was the main source of teaching, through its monasteries and cathedral schools. Originally established for the clergy or those preparing to enter some form of religious life, the curriculum was gradually broadened and such schools were able to include lay pupils, mainly from wealthy backgrounds. The development of the universities followed, once again catering for the educational/spiritual needs of those with wealth and/or influence. Occasionally, basic education was provided by parish priests for the children of the poor, but it was not until the early modern era, when basic literacy levels were dramatically widened by virtue of the emergence of the printing press, that systems of voluntary elementary education were established by various religious and charitable bodies.

Among the most important of these were the early circulating schools in Wales established by, for example, Griffith Jones of Llanddowror, Methodist cleric and educational reformer.[2] It is not known when these schools originally commenced, but in 1737 there were 37 schools with 2,400 pupils. These schools were held for three-monthly periods in the same place, and usually during the winter when farm work was not so pressing. Evening classes were also held for those unable to attend during the day. In two generations these had 'established a high degree of literacy among the people.'[3] Most of those attending these schools were, of course, children, but it is evident that they were also meant to meet the needs of adults for, in 1738, Griffith Jones declared that 'the benefit of hired servants, day labourers, and married men and women... is intended by them'.[4] The success of his classes ensured that a substantial number of literate persons existed who were willing and able to transfer their skills to succeeding generations. Here, then, we have a blueprint for lifelong learning that was adhered to when such education became formalised under the aegis of the universities. Education was being taken to the people, vocational training linked to the job market ran in tandem with non-vocational, but personally fulfilling, education, and those so trained were able and often willing to pass on their knowledge to others, an example which was to be later followed by the University in its community outreach initiatives. The authors of a *Survey of Adult Education in Wales* (prepared by the University's Extension Board in 1940) observed that:

> The cumulative effect of such a development was that between 1800 and 1850 the inhabitants of Wales had at their disposal facilities for Adult Education which in many respects would satisfy the official requirements of the present day. In academic standards only would this activity, in common with most of the cultural efforts of the early nineteenth century, fail to satisfy contemporary requirements.[5]

The thirst for education affected the whole of Wales and in the early days was more powerful in country districts than in industrialised centres. Sunday schools (both rural and urban) soon followed the circulating schools and were ultimately adopted by all religious denominations. The Sunday school brought with it a sense of formality and community. The meetings were regular, lessons were prepared beforehand, syllabuses were drafted and small numbers of Sunday schools often grouped together. Although these schools were democratic in ethos, their powerful religious affiliations meant that they did not always acknowledge and embrace the 'freedom of enquiry and discussion' that would become such a valued feature of later, university-driven adult education.[6]

The process of industrialisation coupled with the enthusiasm for adult education created a demand for suitable literature – and the Welsh press responded accordingly. In 1850 their publication output included fifteen quarterly, two bi-monthly, one hundred monthly, eleven fortnightly and four weekly magazines (almost all in the English language). As Henry Richard, a contemporary local MP, indicated at the time 'The greater part of the issues are taken by the working classes, miners, workers in slate quarries, artisans, small farmers, and agricultural labourers.'[7]

Indeed, Henry Richard (1812-1888) had a lifelong interest in educational reform. Trained for the Congregationalist ministry, he ceased to use the title reverend in about 1853, though he remained attached to the denomination. A member of the Peace Society, of the Liberation Society and a champion of Welsh interests he became MP for Merthyr in the 1868 election, holding the seat until his death. In 1880 he was a member of the departmental committee established under Lord Aberdare to investigate the state of intermediate and higher education in Wales. This committee's recommendations led to the Intermediate Education Act (Wales) of 1889 and to the subsequent establishment of the University of Wales in 1893.[5]

Formal technical adult education in Cardiff began as early as September 1841 when a Mechanics Institute was established. Very little seems to have been recorded of its work and it soon ran into difficulty. It was reconstituted in March of 1848 as Cardiff Athenaeum and Mechanics Institute and is believed to have closed down finally in 1856. It is by no means certain exactly where its premises were located, one source suggesting it was in Church Street in 1851, while another indicates it was based in High Street in 1852.[6]

The next development was the establishment, by public subscription, of a Free Library which for about 2 years was housed in a large room on the present site of the Royal Arcade. The Public Libraries Act of 1855 was adopted by the Burgesses of Cardiff in September 1862, and they took over this existing library. By 1864 it had moved to a building in St Mary Street (originally built for the Young Men's Christian Association), which provided a news room, a magazine room, a library of some 7-8,000 volumes, and a museum on the upper floor.[7] One of the objects of the Public Libraries Act was the establishment of Science and Art Schools, and a resolution was passed at a public meeting held in 1865 recommending the provision of such facilities in Cardiff for which the Libraries Committee was totally responsible. This same Act made it possible to levy a rate for library purposes, including the provision of instruction in science and art. But the amount of money so generated was small (between £400 and £500 for many years) and had to be distributed amongst the Library, the School and the Museum.[8] The fourth Annual Report (1865-66) of the Cardiff Free Library, Museum and Science and Art Schools recorded that 'the schools which were commenced in accordance with this recommendation have been in successful operation for nine months, and bid fair to attain permanent success.'[9] Any person who was successful in passing one of the Science and Art Department's certificate of competency examinations could, if approved by the Department, establish themselves as a teacher for that particular subject, and their wages were determined by the success of their pupils.

Conditions for both teaching and learning were poor, and students were obliged to use improvised desks produced with the aid of barrels and planks of wood. Nevertheless, rapid growth of the School prompted a removal from St. Mary Street to rented rooms in the Royal Arcade, where they were domiciled for twelve years. One of these rooms later became the restaurant of David Morgan Ltd, one of Cardiff's department stores, now sadly closed. The company was evidently proud of the premises' educational past because it erected a commemorative plaque above the restaurant fireplace, stating 'The School of Science and Art, now the Technical College, was established in this room 1st July 1870, and remained here to 24th July 1882'. The prestigious nature of the school was further emphasised by the fact that one of its ex-pupils, Sir William Goscombe John, went on to become an internationally renowned sculptor (John had attended art classes at the Cardiff school for some years before moving to London in 1881).[10] One further move took place, to the library building in The Hayes in 1882, before the work was taken over by the new University College at which point a new symbiotic relationship was born and our story really begins.

In the beginning: the origins of Cardiff University's community outreach mission

Cardiff University, or the University of South Wales and Monmouthshire as it was originally known, owes its establishment indirectly to the Report (August 1881) of a departmental committee which was initiated by W E Gladstone's Liberal government. This departmental committee consisted of Lord Aberdare (Chairman), Viscount Emlyn, MP, the Reverend Prebendary Robinson (of York), Mr Henry Richard, MP (mentioned above), Professor John Rhys, and Mr Lewis Morris, member of Aberystwyth College Council, and its terms of reference were as follows:

> To inquire into the present condition of Intermediate
> and Higher Education of Wales, and to recommend the
> measures which they may think advisable for improving and
> supplementing the provision that is now, or might be made,
> available for such education in the Principality.[11]

The Report, which was highly regarded, recommended '...the establishment of one college,' to be partly supported by a Parliamentary grant of £4,000 per annum, 'in Glamorganshire for South Wales'. The Report also anticipated that ' ...there might be some difference of opinion as to the rival claims of Cardiff and Swansea to be regarded as the most suitable site.' Such a struggle between the two towns did in fact become a reality. In a move to secure the selection of Cardiff, a public meeting was held in the town on 11th January 1882. Enthusiasm was such that donations amounting to £7,250 were that day promised towards the establishment of a university in Cardiff. This was followed on 13th February 1882 by a memorial which was forwarded to the Right Honourable The Earl Spencer, KG, Lord-President of the Council on Education, by the Mayor, Aldermen and Burgesses of the Borough of Cardiff, drawing his attention to the 'special and important claims of the borough of Cardiff to the establishment of the College in Glamorgan at Cardiff.'[12] The committee which prepared this memorial comprised about two hundred persons and represented the interests of all classes in the community. Despite its large size, the whole committee was authorised to present its memorial to the Board of Education, and apparently a special train was provided for the journey of the members to London on 3rd November 1882.[13] Much discussion and correspondence ensued and it was eventually agreed, on the advice of the Vice-President of the Council on Education (the Right Honourable A J Mundella), that the matter should be determined by arbitration. Three arbitrators – Lord Carlingford, Lord Bramwell and Mr Mundella, MP – were acknowledged by the two camps and their decision was as follows:

> We hereby determine and award that Cardiff become the site of the College intended to be established and endowed in South Wales. This decision is unanimous.
>
> March 14, 1883. Carlingford, Bramwell, A J Mundella[14]

It was not until some nineteen months later, on 7th October 1884, that the University was granted a Royal Charter by Queen Victoria. Nevertheless, despite the fact that it lacked an official charter until this date, the University had opened its doors in earnest on 24th October 1883 catering not only for full-time residential day students but also for part-time evening students too. This was due in no small measure to the enthusiasm of those who supported and promoted the College. Some preparation for the establishment of a University had been made as far back as August 1882 when a committee of eighteen members[15] was elected to draw up a plan for the founding and administration of the proposed institution.[16] In preparing their scheme in the form of a draft, the main features of Cardiff's founding Charter were determined. This would be a 'democratic institution – a College for the people, controlled by the people – open equally to men and women without invidious distinctions of any kind and free from all taint of sectarianism.'[17]

However, the prospect of such a democratic institution did not meet with the approval of all. One fundamental condition of the Charter proved to be particularly contentious. This stated:

> ...no student, professor or teacher, or other officer or person connected with the college shall be required to make any declaration as to his religious opinions or to submit to any test whatsoever thereof and that no gift or endowment for theological religious purposes or having any theological conditions attached thereto shall be accepted on behalf of the college.

This clause clearly antagonised certain influential ecclesiastical figures. In August of 1884 the University Registrar wrote to Lord Aberdare and commented:

> Saw Bishop of Llandaff today ...judging from what he says ...I am inclined to think a determined course of action antagonistic to the college has been fixed upon by the Clericals Party.[18] The Bishop said he hoped to live to see the Cardiff College an unmitigated failure.[19]

The secular nature of the University charter was to remain a bone of contention for some time. More significantly, the second paragraph of the Charter contains a crucial commitment to adult education, community engagement and what we now call 'widening access' stating that it was the University's clear mission ' ...to promote higher education generally by providing for persons who are not matriculated students, instruction in the form of lectures combined with class teaching and examining, at such places and in such subjects as shall be determined from time to time.'[20]

This was a particularly progressive clause and has very few contemporary parallels. Its position of prominence within the

University Charter's opening section must almost certainly be attributed to the influence of Dr R D Roberts (1851-1911) an early pioneer and passionate champion of adult education, especially in Wales.[21]

Given its poor financial situation, the task ahead of the University was not an easy one and lack of suitable premises was probably one of the most worrying aspects. However, after some discussion (and much disagreement) with the Town Council it was finally agreed that the University should rent the Old Infirmary premises in Newport Road on a yearly tenancy at six months' notice at a cost of £400 a year, the college to pay all repairs, rates and taxes.[22] These premises were described by one former student, Edith Williams, as 'so inadequate that there were sheds with corrugated roofs dotted all over the grounds, and which were anything but rain-proof,'[23] an opinion shared by novelist Howard Spring and expressed in his autobiographical novel 'Heaven Lies About Us' (1939): 'Evening classes were held in the University College, a hotch-potch collection of wooden shacks surrounding a building that had once been an hospital. They were good classes. Many of them were conducted by the professors of the University seeking some small addition to what they could earn by day.'[24]

It is worth digressing, at this point, to examine Spring's personal experience. Howard Spring had a hard, yet fascinating, background which epitomises both the barriers faced by what we now call non-traditional learners and indeed the life-changing nature of higher education more generally. Born in Canton, Cardiff on 10th February 1889, he was the third of the nine children of William and Mary Spring. William, a jobbing gardener who had fled his home in County Cork as a boy, was often out of work, while Mary took in washing to help support the family. As a consequence of his father's premature death, Howard left school (reluctantly) at twelve, and had a few jobs before discovering a lifelong vocation in journalism and writing. Indeed, his distinguished journalistic career flourished from very humble origins as a messenger boy for the South Wales News where he spent nine years. His energy and commitment to writing were such that he began the '…laborious process of self-education… '[25] Motivated by his desire to become a reporter, he mastered shorthand and so impressed his Cardiff editor that his tuition fees were paid to enable him to study English,

French, Latin, mathematics and history at part-time evening classes held by Cardiff University. In 1912 he moved to Bradford to work on the *Yorkshire Observer* where he began to specialise in reviewing books. He saw service during the World War One and secured an impressive journalistic post with the *Manchester Guardian* for whom he worked for many years. He did not begin writing novels until he was in his forties; nevertheless, his third novel *O Absolom* (retitled *My Son, My Son* for the American market), first published in 1938, was internationally successful and especially well received in the United States where it was eventually adapted into a Hollywood movie.[26] Spring's success brought him considerable wealth and prestige in his middle-age and he continued to write and publish successfully until his death in 1965.

By the end of August 1884, shortly before Cardiff University received its Royal Charter, 151 full-time undergraduate students and 700 part-time evening-class students were already being educated there.[27] At this time, almost all professorial and lecturing staff were 'under contractual obligation to lecture in the towns and countryside as well as in the colleges.'[28] This meant that subjects available to full-time undergraduates were also available for part-time external students both in Cardiff and further afield. Furthermore, a staggering array of extra-mural courses were on offer for these part-time learners including: literature, theology, philosophy, history, astronomy, chemistry, electricity, geology, physics and botany.

Cardiff's early 'lifelong learning' and 'widening access' initiatives proved to be very popular indeed. In 1884-5, the Vice-President of the Council on Education observed that 'students whose early education has been neglected have come in very considerable numbers'.[29] The University Registrar, Ivor James, took great pride in the fact that with a 66% pass rate for matriculation candidates, Cardiff had done better than London – whose rate was only 50%. Indeed, his pride in this achievement prompted him to write to the editor of *Telegraphic Journals* on the subject on 30th August. Yet, in spite of such successes the University's early financial state was such that in August/ September of 1884 a memorandum was sent to the Lords Commissioners of Her Majesty's Treasury indicating that 'in its present financial circumstances the University Council would have the greatest difficulty in providing the sum of £250 for stamp duties and fees payable in connection with the grant of a Royal Charter.'[30] Fortunately, on the 23rd September 1884, a letter from Treasury Chambers indicated that their Lordships would be pleased to authorise the remission of all public fees due for the Charter.[31] This was welcome news indeed, although the University was to remain impoverished for some time to come, partly due to the fact that promised independent funding was not forthcoming:

> ...the town and the Marquess of Bute were slow to deliver on their promises of £10,000. So in their lesser way were many others. After eight years, less than half the promised money had actually been paid.[32]

Whilst full-time student fees are a matter of record, so far no information has come to light regarding fees charged to students for attendance at evening classes. They must have been modest or they would have been unlikely to attract 700 students in the Cardiff area alone during the first year. It is therefore tempting to speculate that they were kept artificially low and that the college suffered a financial loss as a result. Moreover, the dilemma, faced in these early years, of balancing funding and tuition fees with the imperative to provide an inclusive quality adult education programme continues to have a powerful resonance for the lifelong learning sector in our own times.

'Widening Access' in the Victorian Era: the University Extension Movement – 1883-1914

The University Extension Movement originated in Cambridge in the early 1870s inspired by the educational reformer and politician James Stuart (1843-1913) in response to pressures from women demanding access to education. Educated at St Andrew's University and Trinity College, Cambridge, he was a supporter of Josephine Butler's North of England Council for Promoting the Higher Education of Women. He had a chequered political career, and continued his association with Josephine Butler by assisting in the campaign for the repeal of the Contagious Diseases Acts. He was a vigorous advocate of female suffrage and of reform of the House of Lords. His plethora of interests also included journalism, and he was editor of the *Star* and *Morning Leader* from 1890 to 1898. Although he was not the sole originator of the University Extension Movement, he certainly distinguished himself as its most prominent early activist.[33] Stuart clearly regarded the initiative as an opportunity to forge an educational institution that would give equal access to all classes and both sexes. The Extension Movement aimed to place university teachers' services at the disposal of the general community as distinct from their often privileged residential undergraduate students. The movement expanded in the first ten years, eventually reaching the Welsh border when a course was arranged at Welshpool in 1874. By September 1875 the Cambridge Extension initiative reached Cardiff with a number of free inaugural lectures acting as 'tasters' for a series of successful short courses in subjects such as English literature, physical geography and geology.[34] Further courses were to follow between 1875 and 1882. These included topics as diverse as political economy, chemistry and drama. It must be acknowledged that the success of these extension courses was somewhat erratic; enrolment numbers fluctuated dramatically, funding was sparse and on several occasions lecturers failed to show up to teach advertised classes. Nonetheless, the Cambridge extension lectures clearly acted as a catalyst for the establishment of a local higher education institution in the city. Thus when Cardiff University came into being in 1883-4, it immediately established its own extension lecture initiative, with twelve evening courses at the University itself as well as courses at Newport, Merthyr Tydfil and Pontypridd. The following year saw courses established at Llanelli, Swansea, Penarth and Ystrad. Yet, the period 1885-86 was to witness a significant decline in the University's nascent extra-mural provision which was reduced to just two courses in that academic year (this was followed by a very slight improvement in the 1886-7 session when four courses were run). Thus the University's idealistic community engagement operation soon fell on hard times with funding and staffing deficiencies dictating that only the most popular lectures might proceed.[35]

It must be acknowledged that the cessation of such courses was not confined to Cardiff; Aberystwyth and Bangor discontinued their courses by the end of the nineteenth century. It was at this time (1896) that the University of Wales was established, and it has been suggested that internal lecturing demands, together with responsibility for its own examinations and a great increase in committee work led to their demise.[36] This was a great loss to those early adult learners who had enthusiastically participated in the courses which all of the Welsh Universities had offered.

Another contributing factor to the University's faltering adult education/community engagement initiative was that in 1892 county councils obtained powers to provide technical courses under the Department of Science and Art and, in South Wales, these powers were used. County Council classes 'became the recognised means of enabling students to qualify for technical posts and especially for the teaching profession.'[37] The *Survey of Adult Education in Wales* suggests that

> ...the direction which University policy took in the nineties meant that adult education work in Wales continued

fragmentarily and with no unifying spirit and purpose until
a new opportunity occurred in the constitution of the
Extension Board of the University of Wales in 1919.'[38]

Yet, the contemporary sources that are extant do challenge this view,
albeit to a limited extent. Whilst there is no doubt that the County
Councils were responsible for the technical provision (in a co-operative
scheme with the University), a wish to supplement this with a more
cultural provision was expressed by several pioneers of University
Extension in Cardiff: Professor J S Mackenzie (1860-1935), Professor
Ronald Burrows (1867-1920) and Professor A G Little (1863-1945), all
key figures in the history of Cardiff's lifelong learning provision.[39]

Professor Mackenzie was orphaned as a small boy whilst his family
were in South America. Consequently he was cared for by relatives
in the town of his birth, Glasgow. A brilliant student at Glasgow
University, he was awarded a fellowship at the University of Edinburgh,
where he took up the subject of social philosophy. He proceeded to
Trinity College, Cambridge in 1886 where he was eventually elected
into a fellowship. Appointed Professor of Logic and Philosophy at
Cardiff University in 1895, he retired in 1915 in order 'to have time
to write.' He was elected a fellow of the British Academy in 1934.
The background of Professors Little and Burrows will subsequently
be discussed more fully.

In 1901, these liberally-minded academics persuaded the College
Senate to set up a University Extension Committee. The *Centenary
History of Cardiff University* of 1983 comments that these individuals
expended 'strenuous efforts' towards Cardiff's community engagement
initiatives between 1902 and 1912 yet observes that these efforts met
with only 'limited, sporadic success.'[40] Generally speaking this may
constitute a reasonable assessment with regard to the extension lecture
initative. Yet it ignores completely the significant collaboration activities
of the University and the council-run Technical College during this
period. The Technical Instruction Act of 1889 empowered authorities
to establish technical schools and to levy rates for the development of
technical education by the establishment of local technical schools and

colleges.[41] Co-operation with adjacent authorities in order to spread costs was also permitted, if necessary, and Cardiff quickly seized the opportunity on offer and in 1889 appointed a Technical Instruction Committee.[42] This Committee included members of the Corporation (ie, Cardiff Borough Council), representatives of the University College of South Wales and Monmouthshire (ie, Cardiff University), and local industrialists.

The accommodation of the classes of the Science and Arts Schools (later Technical College) in Cardiff's Library Building (mentioned above) had become inadequate and negotiations began with the Council of the comparatively new University College. The result was that the University agreed to provide both teaching venues and teachers in exchange for an annual payment. It was almost certainly a reflection of the University's dire financial situation that (given the poor state of their own teaching accommodation) they were agreeable to such an arrangement. 'In effect the borough council 'farmed out' work to the college.'[43] So it came to be that evening classes in commerce, housewifery, music, science and technology were conducted on the University premises, whilst a certain number of art classes were held during the daytime. As the teaching provision increased in volume, the University was prompted to buy the old Cardiff Proprietary School in Dumfries place as a centre for these technical and other non-university classes.[44] It was certainly no coincidence that, during the period 1890 until 1901, the University's College Principal, John Viriamu Jones, also acted as the Principal of this affiliated Technical School.

In 1906/07, Sir Philip Magnus,[45] examined the educational work of the Corporation and prepared a critical report entitled 'The School System of Cardiff, with special reference to the provision of Evening Technical Instruction and the Agreements between the Corporation and the University Council.' It is worth quoting from this enquiry as it clearly illustrates the pragmatic 'deal' that had been struck between the University and the Technical College:

> ...in September 1890, the Corporation of the County Borough of Cardiff agreed to make an annual payment of £2,500 to the Council of the College, to include rent, rates,

taxes and maintenance etc., of such of the College buildings
as were to be placed at the disposal of the Corporation for
the purposes of Evening Technical Instruction, as well as
for interest on capital expended in erecting new buildings, to
be approved by the Corporation, the use of apparatus and
teaching appliances, and the salaries of the teaching staff,
including a portion of the Principal's remuneration. All fees
and grants were to be retained by the College Council, which
was made responsible for the conduct of a Technical and Art
School, in accordance with the requirements of the Technical
Instruction Committee of the Borough Council.[46]

Sir Philip subsequently concluded that both 'educationally and financially
the arrangements were unduly complicated and unsatisfactory, and that
they were militating against the proper organisation and development of
the work.'[47] He therefore recommended that the existing arrangements
be terminated and a new scheme devised. This task fell to a Mr Charles
Coles who, in 1907, was appointed as Superintendent of Technical
Education, to supervise this form of education on behalf of the
town council, and the University's role in this strand of community
engagement was to diminish thereafter.

During the early years of the twentieth century the University
extension lectures were to find a new lease of life thanks especially to
the efforts of Professor A G Little, Cardiff University's first designated
lecturer in history. Little, the second son of a Buckinghamshire curate
was born at Marsh Gibbon, Buckinghamshire in 1863. He received
a good education at preparatory school in Folkestone and Clifton
College before entering Balliol College, Oxford in 1882 where he
obtained a first class degree in modern history. After several years of
private research he was appointed at Cardiff in 1892. Little had a great
interest in both local history and medieval life and did a great deal to
establish Cardiff's reputation for historical research. He was to resign
late in 1901 due to his wife's ill health and his efforts to re-establish
the University's extension programme may well have been motivated
by his desire to leave Cardiff with a lasting legacy. Certainly, upon his
death he was regarded as 'a sincere, upright and gifted man of unselfish

kindness.'[48]

On 1st February 1901, A G Little sent a letter to members of staff at Cardiff regarding a proposed revival of the University extension scheme. The letter was clearly intended to test the waters regarding the viability and collective will for regenerating the scheme. It suggested that a fee of £1 1s 0d per lecture be paid to tutors, a rate which was lower than that paid by the London, Oxford, Cambridge or Victoria (Manchester) extension schemes. Little feared that the scheme would not be successful if costs were any higher. He did, however, propose that extra fees would be paid to tutors for providing papers or examinations and they would also receive travelling expenses. His letter also included a searching questionnaire which asked questions such as:

> 'Are you willing to give lectures on these terms next session?'
> 'How many courses (from 4-12)?'
> 'Can you suggest names of past students of college who would be competent to lecture on your subject?'
> 'Any persons who might prove efficient secretaries and organisers in the different centres?'[49]

Little made it clear that every effort should be made to establish external community outreach centres for teaching at many of the populous towns in South Wales, including Cardiff, Swansea, Newport, Merthyr, Barry, Neath, Bridgend, Brecon and Aberdare.[50] He must have received a good response to his appeal because barely a month later (13th March 1901) he circulated a very similar letter to potential tutors on his list who were not members of the University staff. In the hope of attracting a dedicated pool of part-time teachers he enthused that:

> The value of such work as is contemplated needs no emphasising, and it is felt by many that the higher educational movement in Wales is now sufficiently old, and has been sufficiently successful to enable this college, and the Welsh University to extend more widely, their sphere of influence. From this information a preliminary list of lecturers and subject will be drawn up and

published with the Extension Prospectus, if approved by the college.[51]

In a nod towards the University's democratic and secular founding principles, he noted that whilst lectures in Welsh were most welcome, Biblical subjects should not be included. He also observed that the list of lecturers was very weak on the science side, and that new members of staff in science-based disciplines should be invited to become extension lecturers as they might supply requirements which the published list of lectures did not meet (for example, Haverfordwest were anxious to have a tutor who could lecture on electricity). Teaching quality was considered to be very important and new lecturers would be required to give a test lecture before they were appointed. The suggested audiences for such trial lectures included schools, women's institutes, the YMCA, and the Working Man's Debating Society.

An Extension Committee was subsequently appointed to deal with Little's proposed 'lifelong learning' programme. It comprised of Professor A G Little himself (History), Professor J S Mackenzie, (Logic and Philosophy), Professor W N Parker (Biology), and Professor S J Chapman (Political Science) and their deliberations led to Senate reporting the findings to Council on 23rd April 1901. The general lack of success in the University's previous community outreach initiatives was attributed to two key areas at this time. Firstly, that permanent academic teaching staff were not able to devote sufficient time to extra-mural lecturing and, secondly, that the expense of setting up extension lectures had been too great for all but the largest towns in the region. Nevertheless, it was envisaged that the extension scheme, at this time, was far better placed to make a recovery and to thrive because the pool of potential tutors was now far greater, thanks to the significant number of competent and professional ex-university students or alumni who continued to reside in the region and who were more than willing to pass on their acquired knowledge and skills. It was therefore anticipated that this, together with a reasonably attractive lecture fee of one guinea, would solve the previous problems of heavy staff work loads and recruitment.

Copies of the Prospectus of University Extension Lectures for the session October 1901, to March 1902 and for the following year still exist and, because of the clarity in setting out its 'widening access' credentials the associated General Regulations need little interpretation. Consequently they are quoted here *verbatim*.

I OBJECTS

The object of the University Extension Movement is to provide instruction in University Subjects for those who cannot come to the University, and to develope (*sic*) the interest of the public in history, literature, art, the social and natural sciences, and philosophy, by means of popular lectures.

II GENERAL ARRANGEMENTS

Before the College can enter into any arrangement with a particular locality [ie, establish an outreach centre] the following conditions must be fulfilled:

1. A Local Committee must be appointed, with a Secretary to correspond with the College. This may be either –
    (a) A Committee specially formed for the purpose; or
    (b) A public educational body, such as a School Board, or a Technical Education, or Library Committee of a County, District, or Town Council; or
    (c) The Committee of some other organized institution, *e.g.* a Literary or Scientific Society, Mechanics' Institute, Working Men's Club, Co-operative Society, etc.

2. A fund sufficient to cover the College charges must be raised or guaranteed by the Local Committee, who will be responsible for the same.

III COST

The fee to Lecturers this Session will be at the rate of One

Guinea for each lecture. The Local Committee will also defray the travelling expenses of the lecturer, and any expenses incurred in illustration of the lectures, as well as all incidental expenses, such as hire of hall, lighting, attendance, and advertising.[52]

Copies of the above prospectus were sent to a large number of possible centres across South Wales.[53] Included on the mailing lists were ministers of religion, head teachers and teachers, doctors and chemists, Justices of the Peace, librarians, secretaries of technical institutes and working men's institutes, women's institutes, etc. In fact, anyone of social standing who was possibly willing and able to arrange evening classes in their area and, more importantly, to arouse the enthusiasm of its citizens. The University became affiliated to the Workers' Educational Association in 1906, a few years after it was founded (1903), at a fee of one guinea and added their organisation to the growing list of co-operating bodies. The Prospectus reveals only those lectures given in Cardiff and, as would be expected, a large percentage of such courses were given there by the University's own lecturing staff. These embraced both arts and sciences and included such widely disparate subjects as: The Principles of Hygiene, Some National Heroes (Julius Caesar, Napoleon Buonaparte, Nelson, Bismark), Light and Colour (illustrated) and The Duties of Citizenship.[54]

Enormous credit is due to the staff of the University Extension Movement at this time. They taught full-time students by day, part-time students at night, and organised and largely ran the Technical College for the Borough, based mostly in sub-standard accommodation. Arguably, the same could be said for those lecturers engaged in other towns/villages in South Wales. They too must have pursued day-time occupations before lecturing at night, as indeed do most modern-day tutors.

The records show that from 1902 to 1905 courses were delivered at a staggering thirty-two different centres across South East Wales. Unfortunately, from 1906 onwards only the number of lectures was reported making it harder to identify the geographical spread, the highest figure of sixty lectures appearing in 1905-06. By 1908-09 it had dropped dramatically to just four, though a 'somewhat unstable revival' occurred in 1912-13 when seventeen lectures were delivered.[55] Yet, although the members of the University Extension Committee were deeply committed to the cause and made huge efforts to maintain and develop the enterprise, understandably, their work was to all but collapse with the onset of World War One in 1914.

The University Settlement in Splott

A further significant community engagement initiative emerged in Cardiff during the early years of the twentieth century which ran concurrently with the Extension Scheme – the Cardiff University Settlement. Its lifespan was not inordinately long and yet its importance in bridging the gap between social classes in the city was invaluable, following as it did Cardiff's 'inclusive' community mission as stated in its original Charter.

The University Settlement movement originally came into being when, in 1884, Samuel and Henrietta Barnett, friends of the social reformer and political economist, Arnold Toynbee, established Toynbee Hall in the Whitechapel district of London in order to celebrate his life and work. Both a student and a tutor at Oxford, Toynbee's lectures dealt with the principles of economics and contemporary economic history, but his main interest was in the dramatic socio-economic upheavals instigated by the industrial revolution between the middle of the eighteenth century and his own time.[56] It was felt by many that industrialisation had formed a chasm between rich and poor, a chasm that was difficult to breach. Historically the two had been geographically, if not economically, close but industrialisation had brought large numbers of the rural poor into urban areas, and at the same time driven the rich out of urban centres into country estates. The Settlement ideal was to create a centre where holidaying students from Oxford and Cambridge Universities could link 'town and gown' by working among, and hopefully improving, the lives of, the poor.[57] There is no doubt that this work was commendable and did much to alleviate the pressures of poverty, but altruism was not the only motive. Large numbers of poor people congregating in slums were regarded as a threat to law and order and education was prescribed as one possible antidote to the perceived rift in social order created by industrialisation and urbanisation. One contemporary provided the following description in an investigation into the condition of the riverside population in London:

> I venture to afflict your ears with a very brief description of that part of London. You will believe me when I assure you that I am not able – simply not able – to set forth the whole truth, or anything like the whole truth… The people, taken as a whole, were the most abandoned and dissolute ever known. Every man of the stevedores, of the barge and lightermen, of the boatmen, was a robber and a thief: All together daily plundered the cargoes of the ships. They robbed the cargoes of big things; they stole little things; every day they went ashore with the goods they stole; every house was a receiving-house and a tavern. The men spent their unholy gains in drink. Their children grew up without the least tincture of education, in an atmosphere of crime and drunkenness; while of virtue, modesty, honesty, there was not a trace.[58]

Similar concerns are evident in other contemporary surveys including *The Universities and the Social Problem*. In the first chapter, the Right Honourable Sir John Gorst MP observed that:

> …modern civilization has certainly had the effect of concentrating the destitute classes, and of making their existence thereby more conspicuous and dangerous… But the evil may be on the increase. Almost every winter in London there is a panic lest the condition of the poor should become intolerable. The richer classes awake for a moment from their apathy and salve their consciences by a subscription of money… The annual alarm may some day prove a reality, and the destitute classes may swell to such proportion as to render the continuance of our existent social system impossible.[59]

The tangible fear of social disorder clearly permeates these two, obviously prejudiced, accounts. In his study *Intellectual Life of the British Working Classes,* Rose has observed that the history of education with its theme of social control has been written mainly from the perspective of the suppliers of education rather than with its consumers.[60] By shifting attention to the students, we may get a totally different picture and, in the absence of student records from the early days, one area that immediately springs to mind is the University Settlement, a movement that united education and paternalistic social care. The key figure in the University Settlement at Cardiff was Ronald Burrows, Professor of Greek from 1898 to 1908 who, as we saw earlier, was also heavily involved in the establishment of the University's extension lectures.[61] Born in 1867 at Rugby (where his father, the Reverend L F Burrows was a housemaster) he was educated at Oxford. His family was well endowed with men of the church and he married the daughter of a bishop. His political leanings were Tory but he embraced Christian socialism and was active as a social reformer. It was in the autumn of 1901 that both Professor and Mrs Burrows, aided by Professor S J Chapman and Professor J S Mackenzie[62] (Treasurer of the Settlement), Miss Lilian Howell (a former University College student who was secretary of the Settlement from 1901 to 1907), and others founded the Cardiff Settlement.[63] They sought advice from the Chief Constable of Cardiff as to which area would be suitable for such work and he suggested the East Moors of Splott – an area identified by him as being one where poverty was the norm because of the casual nature of employment, exacerbated by drinking and gambling. They began their work in a few club rooms in 50 and 52 Portmanmoor Road, Splott[64] 'where the lads and the staff of officers and helpers met night after night for instruction in various trades and branches of knowledge, for games, and for each other's society.' Lord Tredegar was the honorary president of the club, and many other prominent people took a practical interest in the work, including Mr Charles Thompson (the Thompson family were flour merchants in Cardiff – Spillers Flour Mill), Sir Alfred Thomas MP (later Lord Pontypridd), Mr Raymund Allen, Mr Anton Bertram (later Sir Anton Bertram, Chief Justice of Ceylon),

Mr J C Dore (Cardiff University), Mrs Alfred Thomas (probably Lady Pontypridd) who later succeeded Miss Howell as Secretary, Mr A J Wade-Gery, a Cardiff University lecturer, and other junior members of the college staff. A Lads' Club was run by Mrs Burrows, a Women's Club by Miss Howell, a Girls' Club by a Miss Baker and a Men's Club by Mr Dore. The two shops rented at 50 and 52 Portmanmoor Road, underwent structural alterations and the building was adapted and named University House. 'A caretaker was appointed, pianos bought, ping-pong, billiards, and other games provided' and the membership averaged two hundred, the Lads' Club having a nightly attendance of seventy to eighty.[65] This gives some indication of the club's popularity. Membership cost a halfpenny a week and this included instructional classes as well as games and members were allowed to attend on three club nights. There were also extra charges, for example one penny for dancing, one penny for the gymnasium, and one penny for billiards. The Women's Club had a cottage at Caerphilly (called *Cuckoo Cottage*) where the cost of a week-end stay was two shillings and four pence, or one shilling and sixpence a day. Smoking concerts cost three pence but this included cigarettes and tobacco. From these details it would appear that the Settlement had very little to do with education and indeed, Professor Burrows himself admitted that 'we do believe that in our clubs we help you to keep steady and straight through the week', and so avoid the pitfalls of public houses and strong drink.[66] However, he also reminded members that in order to avoid these dangers 'we get you to take classes, to keep up what you learnt at school, your reading and writing and arithmetic and to give you the fresh interests of history and citizenship, of engineering and wood-carving, and bent iron work.'[67]

At the time the Settlement was established, Professor Burrows had a desirable official residence at The Lodge, Radyr, but soon gave up these affluent surroundings and moved to 131 Habershon Street in the heart of the Splott district. He could have administered the Settlement from afar, and the fact that he chose to live among the poor would certainly have enhanced his 'street' credibility on both social and religious grounds. This move certainly appealed to the imagination of College students, who celebrated it in a students' song:

That deeds are worth cartloads of speeches
Our 'Varsity Settlement teaches.
Burrows lives in the slums,
And has gamins for chums,
And practises just what he preaches.[68]

That the Settlement fulfilled deep-seated needs in the Splott community is confirmed by its popularity. In June 1903 the gift of half an acre of land at East Moors was made by Lord Tredegar, one-time President of the University College. By 1906, it had outgrown its original home in Portmanmoor Road and expanded to Walker Road, membership totalling over 400. Education, instruction in useful skills, recreation and friendship were on offer for both men and women, boys and girls. In 1906 an Emigration Fund was established to assist boys who wished to emigrate to Canada, Australia etc. The May 1905 issue of *Cap and Gown* (the college magazine) carried an article on the Girls' Club at the Settlement in which the author quotes a girl member's response to an enquiry as to whether she liked the club. Her answer was 'I'd die for it,' suggesting it offered a real oasis then in a desert of poverty.[69] The clubs were open, initially, every Monday and Thursday from 7.00pm-9.30pm (although they eventually opened more frequently) and, for some, they became a sort of surrogate family. Following Professor Burrows's departure from the town,[70] the running of the Settlement passed to Mr E Lewis (a local solicitor and Quaker from Rhiwbina) and his wife. When World War One broke out, some of the boys who became members of the armed forces kept in touch with the Settlement organisers, with each other, and with the Lewis family, who responded in true family fashion by sending parcels of biscuits, cake, Bovril and Woodbines.[71]

A small collection of very short letters and Field Service postcards from some of its former members still exists – several of which were sent from France during World War One. These both identify a few of the lads, and testify to the strong links formed between them and the University Settlement. The letters sometimes voice the hopes and fears, and also the ambitions of these college 'boys' They are usually optimistic, exhibit a reasonable standard of literacy, learned either at their local Board School or at the Settlement, and contain a smattering of French (no doubt learned at a much harder school). Correspondents include John Childs, HMS Dartmouth; J F Cunningham who was at Territorial Camp Headquarters in Colwyn Bay (he was proud to tell that he was soon to be made a sergeant) and Sergeant W J Dunn, Welsh Regiment, who had been in France since the beginning of the war (receiving wounds on at least one occasion) and who discovered another settlement 'old-boy', Enos Skrine, in the same platoon. D McDonald wrote with an embroidered Christmas greeting card, while a second letter from W J Dunn reveals that 'Enos is in hospital – having a rough time of it out here – 3 gas attacks'. Other names include: Gunner James Hawkey, Royal Artillery; D C W (Dai) Luker, Welsh Guards; C Upcott; Fred Spiller; C H G Hook; H J Hosgood and William Miller (whose ship the SS Oldfield Grange was the first ship to circumnavigate South America). Dai Luker was a regular correspondent and it is in his letters that we can see his enthusiasm wane although his patriotism was never in doubt. He had two horses shot from under him and in 1917 was 'at Heaps (Ypres) in B Comp'. He went on to win the Military Medal, an award that was gazetted in a supplement to the *London Gazette* dated 28th September 1917.[72] A sad little mourning card, dated 26th September 1917, is also in the collection, commemorating Harry Hankins, son of George and Rose, 70 Railway Street, Splott, who died 'somewhere in France' where he 'gave his life for home and freedom.'[73]

Professor Burrows's successor as chairman of the Settlement Council was Professor J Mackenzie, who had also been on Professor Little's Extension Committee. In addition, he had been a member of the Settlement Council since the beginning and also honorary treasurer and a worker in the Men's Club. He continued to serve the Settlement until he left Cardiff in 1915. He married Miss Millicent Hughes, who was Cardiff's first woman Professor of Education (1904-15). Professor Millicent Mackenzie was an active member of the Cardiff Women's Suffrage Society and stood unsuccessfully for the University of Wales seat as the Labour candidate in the General Election on 14th December 1918 (the only female Welsh candidate).

Like most social experiments, the Settlement 'had its ups and downs'.

Financial constraints and shortage of staff were endemic and increased with time. Other social movements also acted as a drain. The Women's Suffrage Movement attracted some of the women helpers, while the Men's Club encountered competition from another club which opened in the neighbourhood in 1910: the John Cory Institute. This proved to be of a temporary nature and membership of the Men's Club soon regained its usual strength of about 150 members.[74] Shortly before World War One, a new youth group, the Scout Movement, attracted thousands of British boys and this also had an effect on the Settlement. The solution to this was the formation of the Settlement's own troop – the 6th Cardiff. Although much good work continued to be done in 1914 and 1915, eventually the male clubs became casualties of the war as members gradually left to join the armed forces. The Women's and Girls' Clubs flourished with increased tasks of knitting woollen comforts for soldiers and preparing Christmas parcels for the hundred or so Settlement members serving in the forces. But it was only a matter of time before the Settlement building was requisitioned 'in order to turn it into a hospital for shell-shocked soldiers and nervous cases'.[75] Both the Settlement Hall and the club buildings were used, and about a hundred patients were so accommodated. It had been hoped to resume activities after the war, but scattering of members combined with a lack of any sense of urgency produced an apathy from which it never recovered. By the summer of 1919 the building was empty and it is interesting to note that unoccupied premises were then, as now, vulnerable. Correspondence on the University Settlement buildings indicates that as a result of damage, the Royal Engineers were asked to make it as secure as possible, and a military guard was put in place.[76] In December of 1922 it was resolved that the University Extension initiative be wound up and the property sold. This was done by public auction and, ironically, this 'non-religious' Settlement was acquired by the Roman Catholic Archdiocese of Cardiff, to become St Illtyd's College in 1923. It is perhaps appropriate here to directly quote from B M Bull's much more detailed study of the University Settlement:

> Thus the work of the Settlement ended, but in many ways its influence lived on. It lived on in individuals, for it touched many

lives, enlarging, enlightening and disciplining through its friendly fellowship. It lived on in movements, for together with other settlements it showed ways of satisfying some of the unmet needs of the poor. The adult education movement, the youth movement, and our social welfare services all owe something to the pioneer efforts of settlements such as this.[77]

'War and Peace': developments in Cardiff's community outreach provision –1914-1945

Just as the University Extension Movement was showing great promise, a serious curtailment of the provision occurred during 1915-16 and a complete cessation during 1916-17 due to the demands of World War One. Educational provision in general was 'at a very low ebb' during these years with reduced school hours, lower school leaving age and teacher shortages. Unsurprisingly, adult education was also heavily disrupted, with little being done for the growing captive audiences in military service and munitions factories.[78] This neglect created a public outcry which focussed its efforts on campaigning for educational reform after the war. Consequently a national conference of the Adult Education Committee of the Ministry of Reconstruction, presided over by the Master of Balliol, A L Smith, was held at Balliol College as early as July 1916 to consider the future of education and in particular working-class education. Not surprisingly adult education was stressed and by 1919 the important and highly influential report of this committee was issued.

Generally, this report reaffirmed that during the 1914-1918 conflict educational matters had been of low priority. Nevertheless, it produced evidence suggesting that, independent of the government, a network of voluntary agencies had managed to provide some educational facilities for both civilians and the armed forces during much of this period.[79] The YMCA, working in conjunction with the WEA, the Universities and numerous individuals, set up canteens or 'huts' (social centres) all over the UK and abroad to offer servicemen some of the comforts of home. Education was added to a list of activities quite early in the war and a 'constant series of lectures was arranged, some as far a-field as France, Salonika, Mesopotamia, British East Africa and Malta'.[80] At the request of the army authorities this collective educational association provided university lecturers who paid visits of from 2-4 weeks to troops on the lines of communication in France during the period January to March of 1917 and 1918.[81] They lectured to army schools, special groups of officers and men on a variety of subjects, including literature, history, science and art. Modern languages, particularly French, were a regular popular feature at Base Camp. For instance, at Etaples early in 1918 'over 1,000 men were taking a course in the French language.'[82] However, not everyone in the Forces shared this enthusiasm for adult education. On hearing that a young soldier battalion was about to parade for a history lesson, the Sergeant Major exclaimed scornfully – 'History? History won't kill Germans'.[83]

It has not been possible to identify, specifically, any of the Cardiff University lecturers involved in this scheme but, given the dedication usually exhibited towards adult education by many Welsh academics, it is highly likely that some of Cardiff University men and/or women were among the numbers who willingly gave their services, both on the home front and abroad.

The mood of the nation in 1918 was one of 'post-war euphoria', not least in the sphere of education which has been described as 'a new field of national effort', with particular reference to adult education.[84] The subsequent demand for classes was a product of post-war optimism and idealism; the *Survey of Adult Education in Wales* (published in the 1940s) commented that this: '...led people to desire education as a means by which they could help to create a new order of society among men and among nations.'[85]

This same survey observed that the development of an adult education service capable of establishing classes at almost any centre in Wales was 'essentially a post-war development'.[86] However, it should also acknowledged that the foundations of most of the organizations that made this development possible were actually in place prior to 1918. For example, College (Joint) Committees had been set up at Bangor, Aberystwyth and Cardiff, and a full-time tutor had been appointed for each of these College centres, with a fourth for the Swansea area. Arguably, the experience of the earlier years when money and venues were in short supply was also of value. Moreover, the war years had drained the nation of much of its manpower and associated resources, resulting in a sharpened awareness of the needs of both individuals and the state. A concerted effort was made, involving the government and many education-related movements, in order to redress this situation. The result was a raft of legislation directed towards the provision of quality education for all.

During the period 1918-1924 the provision of grant-earning classes was entirely in the hands of the University Colleges, whilst valuable voluntary work to stimulate the demand for such classes was executed by the WEA and the Workers' Educational Trade Union Committee (WETUC). In 1919 the co-secretaries of the Joint Tutorial Classes Committee, D J A Brown (also Registrar of University College, Cardiff) and John Davies (District Secretary of the WEA in Wales) began to rejuvenate adult education in the region with the number of tutorial classes trebling between 1919 and 1924.[87] Throughout these years both national and local libraries helped to keep costs of adult education down by providing, on loan, boxes of appropriate books. Furthermore, in September 1924, a new set of adult education regulations was established by the Board of Education and these recognized that voluntary associations like the WEA could now run grant-earning classes (a privilege which, as we've seen, was formerly enjoyed only by the university colleges in Wales).[88] In 1923-24 a Joint Advisory Committee for Adult Tutorial Classes was established with Brown and Davies again acting as co-secretaries.

The University continued to suffer financial problems during this time, necessitating reliance on gifts and grants from various sources. Local schools also acted as adult education outreach centres for the University but they did require payment for providing rooms for classes, as well as caretaker fees. The University's funding difficulties were so acute that members of college staff were asked whether they would be prepared to give their services voluntarily in order to deliver a series of lectures. The minutes of the Joint College Tutorial Committee indicates that help was forthcoming with four lecturers offering around fourteen single and/or multiple lectures in a variety of disciplines such, for example Rousseau's *Emile*, Historical Sketch of Foreign Policy,

Production of Fertilizers (see Appendix II).[89] Progress was admittedly quite slow in the immediate post-war years. Yet, despite the industrial unrest of the 1920s, adult education sinitiatives soon gained momentum during the mid-1920s and, by the 1926-27 academic session, 52 classes were organised at Cardiff.[90] During the same decade the Council of Cardiff's University College agreed to accept full responsibility for adult tutorial classes in the area (which brought it into line with the other constituent colleges of the University of Wales).[91]

The inter-war years also witnessed significant numbers of one-off free lectures. The advertising material connected with these 'tasters' comprised some very large posters (2ft x 4-5ft) and a considerable number of smaller 'flyers', suggesting that the lectures were aimed at the public at large as well as the University's full-time and part-time lecturers and students.[92] Once again, D J A Brown was a driving figure, this time in the capacity of Joint Secretary of the University Tutorial Committee a position which he shared with the Cardiff Branch Secretary of the WEA, Mr J C Ashe. Speakers came from other universities too (such as Oxford and Durham), while one was from the Woolwich Arsenal, yet another was assistant editor of the magazine *Nature*. The overall theme was 'Education and Reconstruction after the war', and lecture titles reflect a sense of optimism and determination, as perhaps they were meant to do as a means of post-war propaganda. They included topics such as:

> The National Opportunity
> The British Commonwealth after the War
> Education and the New World
> The Service of the State
> The Commonwealth of Industry
> Good Temper: the First Essential for
>   Reconstruction
> A League of Nations for Peace and International
>   Right
> Science and Industry
> Welfare Work in Industry
> Principles of Reconstruction

The Place of Music in the Life of the Community
State control of Wages
The Arts in Education
Financial Reconstruction
The Art of Listening[93]

Music was also a popular addition to the curriculum and indeed chamber music concerts were a regular feature during the 1920s and 1930s.

During these years, Cardiff University was to work, once again, in collaboration with the YMCA in another community outreach initiative. In 1925, Professor Barbara Foxley of University College, Cardiff, was invited by the Home Office to become the Honorary Adviser in Education, on the women's side, to the Cardiff Prison Governor. The men's side was represented by the Welsh National Secretary of the YMCA, W J Pate. During the early 1920s and beyond there was considerable pressure for change in the prison system, with enlightened thinking on the value of education replacing, at least in part, the old system of punishment. Alexander Paterson (1884-1947), who was appointed as a Prison Commissioner in the early twenties began to reform the prison service.[94] State funds were not available for educational purposes in prisons and so any such work had to be of a voluntary nature. A request for lecturers' services on this basis was favourably received and, although once again the volunteers are not identified, the breadth of subjects offered – ie, Current Affairs, History, English, English Literature, French, Mining, Ambulance Work and Crafts, suggests a mixture of academic, artisan and technical tutors.[95] We do not know to what extent, if any, Cardiff University lecturers were involved in this rehabilitation work. We can only speculate that Professor Foxley may have successfully canvassed her colleagues in this regard. Such educational opportunities would have not only kept prisoners occupied whilst they were incarcerated, but also provide them with useful skills when they were discharged into the community.[96]

It must be noted that the exact moment when the Department

of Extra-Mural studies became an official academic entity at Cardiff University is something of an enigma. Much of the available evidence suggests that this occurred at a relatively late stage, during the post-war era. Indeed, there is little to suggest that the University's community engagement enterprise was allocated its own premises and/or centre of operations much before the early 1950s. Nevertheless, a 'Department of University Extension Lectures' was referred to as early as 1907 when it was described on the back cover of a University Extension Prospectus (though no location was indicated). It is tempting to regard this 'Department' as a somewhat notional institution. Nevertheless, as we have seen, the University became involved in a very large amount of extra-mural work during the 1920s. Moreover, by the early 1930s a Cardiff Department of Extra-Mural Studies had clearly been established even if it had no official premises or designated head.[97] Indeed, it boasted a staff of 33 extra-mural teachers in service who were drawn from within and without the University College.[98] Two full-time 'co-ordinating' tutors were also employed and their pioneering efforts achieved a great deal. By 1935 both tutors received full-time permanent staff status, one gaining the title of 'Organising Tutor for the Monmouthshire/ Breconshire area' with the other similarly occupied for the Glamorgan area.[99]

Notwithstanding the economic depression, the 1930s saw an almost continuous expansion of adult education up to the outbreak of World War Two. By the 1939-40 academic session 64 courses were being arranged by Cardiff University. Although this provision dropped sharply to 53 the following session, only three further courses were lost in 1941-42 indicating 'how little effect the war had so far had on the extra-mural work'.[100] Generally, the quantity and quality Cardiff's adult education provision was maintained during the 1939-45 period, despite the inevitable difficulties that wartime brought. Once again, a clear demand for lectures emanated from the armed forces. Cardiff had a fairly large concentration of troops in the area and a 'very full service of lectures' was provided to their units – ie, 765 single lectures and 30 courses were run during the session 1941-42. Remarkably, throughout the war years, the number of courses provided never fell below the 50 reported in 1941-42 and, in fact, during the last academic session of the war the number rose to 62. This was achieved in addition to the extensive programme provided for the services under the Scheme for University Assistance to Adult Education in HM Forces.[101]

In 1945-6 the University decided to proceed with the appointment of three additional full-time adult education tutors and proposed to appoint a permanent Director of Extra-Mural studies pending funding (although this did not materialise until a few years later). [102] Steps were also taken to strengthen the Department's full-time organising staff and, in 1946/7, two additional organising tutors were appointed. One who, residing in east Monmouthshire, was made responsible for developing the provision in that region, while the second became responsible for the provision in Mid-Glamorgan. Under an expansion plan at the beginning of the 1948-9 session a full-time tutor was appointed for South Breconshire and the Rhymney, Sirhowy and Ebbw Valleys of Monmouthshire. Therefore, by the start of the 1948-9 session the full-time organising staff covered five designated outreach areas.[103]

As already noted, the exact moment when the Department of Extra-Mural Studies acquired its own premises is something of a mystery. The Department's lack of a clear physical location undoubtedly prompted the comment in Chrimes's *Centenary History* that in the early 1950s the 'Department was starting almost from scratch'[104] Yet, the University's vibrant community engagement programme and staffing records appear to suggest otherwise. Indeed, as this study has revealed, Cardiff's extra mural or 'lifelong learning' enterprise can be traced right back to the University's earliest origins during the final quarter of the nineteenth century. In the 1950s the University's extra-mural initiative was finally given a home within the University complex in the shape of a modest one-room 'department' in Corbett Road.[105] It seems clear that no academic would choose to move to a one-room department unless it was better than (or at least equal to) accommodation previously occupied. Therefore, it may well be that before this time the extra-mural provision had continued to be administered centrally by the University Registrar or his assistants; but this does not mean that it didn't exist. Whilst the accommodation allocated to the Department in the 1950s may have been modest, the University's extra-mural enterprise was hardly starting from scratch. It was able to draw upon almost 60 years of community engagement experience. From these modest beginnings in Corbett Road the Department's premises gradually expanded and in the late 1960s it was relocated to a much larger location in the former BBC offices in 38-40 Park Place. This afforded a number of lecture rooms and a reference library. Finally, in 1999 the Department was allocated a building which gave it parity, in size at least, with other significant academic schools within the University, located in Senghenydd Road.

Those at the helm – 1949-2008

Over the past sixty years the Cardiff Centre for Lifelong Learning, as it is now called, has been extremely fortunate, not only in its recruitment of enthusiastic and committed teaching and support staff, but also in having a succession of directors dedicated to the cause of open access adult education and who have worked hard to establish, expand and promote Cardiff University's community engagement undertaking both regionally and indeed nationally. It is therefore appropriate that we complete our study through an examination of the careers of those individuals who grasped the reins and have steered the Centre through periods of success and indeed more turbulent times too. This role call includes D E Evans (Tutor in Charge, 1949-1951), Iwan Morgan (Tutor in Charge, 1951-1965), Leslie Jones (the first Director, 1965-1970), J Selwyn Davies (Director, 1970-1984), John Perkins (Director, 1984-1994), Gill Boden (Acting Director/ Director, 1994-1998), Madeleine Havard (Acting Director, 1998-2000), John King, (Director, 2000-2002) and the current Dean of Lifelong Learning, Dr Richard Evans (2002 onwards). Obituaries penned by Dr Peter Webster are available for Leslie Jones, J Selwyn Davies, John Perkins, and arguably they cannot be bettered. They are, therefore, included, with his permission, in their entirety within this chapter.[106]

D E Evans, Tutor in Charge 1949-1951

D E Evans, a senior and longstanding member of the Department's full-time teaching staff since the 1930s, was appointed as Tutor-in-Charge in 1949, a role he assumed in addition to his duties as organising tutor and extensive teaching responsibilities. Sadly, D E (as he was known to his many friends) died in January 1951 after just two years in post and his passing constituted a 'grievous loss to the Department.'[107] His dedication to adult education in general and the Department in particular knew no bounds and he was respected by all who knew him. At the time of his death the value of the post-war development plan, and the associated demand for adult education, was reflected in the fact that the provision had increased to 96 courses across the region. Also, during D E Evans's brief directorship, a staff tutor, Eric Hodges, was appointed in the subject of music whose responsibilities were to 'organise, conduct and supervise courses in his subject throughout the whole college area – East Glamorgan, Monmouthshire and South Breconshire'[108]

As previously mentioned, music had for some time been part of the curriculum, but this commitment to the discipline in the form of a dedicated member of staff was an important step in the development of the Department's provision. This together with the establishment of the Eric Hodges recitals, a much admired feature of Hodges's work in the Department of Extra-Mural Studies, which began shortly after D E Evans' death in 1951, constitutes a lasting and fitting legacy for his short period at the helm. Following Eric Hodges's death in 1962, a lecture-recital fund was established from subscriptions of his friends, and students of the Department of Extra-Mural Studies, to commemorate the work of this first staff tutor in music.[109] The income from the fund contributes to lecture recitals given annually by instrumentalists of international repute, usually pianists.[110] Indeed, the Eric Hodges recitals have become a significant and enduring event in Cardiff's music calendar. [The latest recital was held on Tuesday 11th December 2007 at the University Concert Hall.][111]

Iwan Morgan, Tutor in Charge 1951-1965

The 1950s and 60s saw more-or-less uninterrupted expansion of the Department's provision under the guidance of Iwan Morgan who served as Tutor-in-Charge during these years. Like D E Evans, Morgan was a longstanding tutor and both taught, organised and directed the Department's adult education provision. During his time in charge he vigorously promoted the Cardiff community outreach mission and introduced innovative ideas, such as celebrity concerts, residential schools and overseas study tours. Publicising the Department proved almost as difficult at this time as it had been in the earliest days of extension lectures some eighty years earlier.

Operating from a one-room department in Corbett Road a circulation list of interested people was drawn up. From this, information was disseminated by word of mouth, aided by a small amount of press advertising. Additionally, annual rallies were held in May of each year, attracting speakers such as Sir Donald Wolfit and Lord Birkett, which drew audiences of up to 1,000 people.[112] Successful evening concerts were also arranged which included leading choirs and bands from the area, as well as those from further afield, for example Ukrainian dancers, a variety of international artists – and even Coco the Clown on one occasion![113] The number of full time teaching staff in the Department remained static at around five for the first ten years of Morgan's leadership but in 1962 he secured the appointment of a staff tutor in biological sciences adding a further important designated discipline to the Department's portfolio. This appointment quickly bore fruit and a vibrant series of courses in biology and the natural sciences was soon established.[114] Sadly, Iwan Morgan passed away during the 1965-66 academic session, yet his 14 years of leadership had laid the foundation of the modern academic department of lifelong learning.'

Leslie Jones 1917-1994 (the first Director, 1965-1970)

Leslie Jones was in many ways typical of a generation of bright Welsh youngsters of the inter-war years. He was born at Tumble in Carmarthenshire and attended the Gwaendreth Valley Grammar School. His university education at Swansea was split by war service in the navy but ultimately resulted in a first in economics in 1947 followed by a lecturing post in Liverpool. He returned to Wales in 1952 to take up the post of Lecturer in Economics at University College, Cardiff and remained in Welsh education thereafter. By the 1960s, he was Senior Lecturer in Economics but suffered illness in the mid 1960s, shortly before being appointed to the new post of Director of Extra-Mural Studies in 1965.

It was widely rumoured that this change from economics to extra-mural studies had more to do with creating what was considered to be an 'easy berth' for Leslie, than it had to do with concern for extra-mural teaching, but undoubtedly he did not see it that way. The post of Director of Extra-Mural Studies was a new one and it undoubtedly helped that Leslie was well known and liked within the internal Departments and the College 'establishment'. The change of direction seems to have brought him a new lease of life. The day-to-day running of the Department was in the very able hands of Harry Clifford but it was the new Director who approved all new classes and who certainly changed the academic direction of its output. Under his leadership, the Department of Extra-Mural Studies increased its complement of full-time subject specialists based in Cardiff with new posts in English literature, psychology and archaeology all appointed during his comparatively brief tenure. The Department moved to premises recently vacated by the BBC among the Victorian villas of Park Place. A single prospectus of winter courses was also instigated.

By the end of the 1960s, Leslie had gathered around him a small but expanding band of young subject tutors and may well have felt that he had successfully changed the face of extra-mural studies. In 1970, he took up a new challenge as secretary of the Welsh Education Board, a post which he held until retirement in 1977. Despite a fondness for gardening, retirement does not seem to have brought much diminution in other activities. He had been a Cardiff JP since 1966. In the late 1970s and 1980s he was to be found on the Council of St David's, Lampeter and of Barnardo's and the Courts of UWIST, the National Library, and the National Museum. He was made an Honorary Fellow of University College Cardiff in 1971.

Leslie Jones died in 1994. He was, in many ways a representative of a body of people, who by the beginning of the twenty-first century, have become an all but vanished breed – the product of the Welsh Grammar School system, educated at a Welsh university and with a strong feeling for their Welsh roots and a willingness to put back a good deal into Welsh education. Despite his comparatively short tenure within the Department of Extra-Mural Studies, he set the course of adult education at Cardiff for the next quarter century and a good many students and staff have good reason to be grateful to him for this. (PVW)

J Selwyn Davies 1921-2000 (Director, 1970-1984)

With the death on (6th April 2000) of John Selwyn Davies, Director of Extra-Mural Studies at University College, Cardiff from 1970 to 1984, the University has lost one of the characters of its pre-merger days. John Selwyn belonged to the inter-war generation whose education was disrupted by World War Two. He went up to Queen's College Oxford in 1939 but remained only a year. From 1940 to 1945 he served in the army. It was in Burma in 1945 that he received the head wound, the evidence of which he carried for the rest of his life. An abiding, if painful, image is of him reading, glasses off and the book held only an inch or two from his one good eye. One cannot but admire the spirit of one who, with such limited vision, returned to Oxford and completed a degree in English as he did in 1948. After Oxford he began what was to be a career in Welsh adult education, firstly at Coleg Harlech, where he rose from Assistant Tutor to Vice-Warden, and then, from 1970, as Director of Extra-Mural Studies at Cardiff. The Cardiff Department when he arrived still had remnants of the pre-war period such as resident tutors in outlying areas. By the time he retired in 1984, it had a complement of full-time, university-based, subject lecturers greater in number than it has ever managed to achieve since. His running of the Department was, at times, idiosyncratic but earned the support of a series of able administrators and he took a keen paternal interest in his largely young academic staff. His patronage of the Staff Club and its bar was legendary, as were his interventions on various College committees.

As with all 'characters' it is easy to remember anecdotal evidence, but this would be to do JSD an injustice. One was not acquainted with him long before one realised that here was an able mind which would probably have 'moved the world' had it not been for an accident of war which robbed him of the easy ability to read. But it might well have been this very fact which led him into adult education and there are many in Wales who owe their 'second start' in education directly or indirectly to him. He will be greatly missed and remembered with affection. (PVW)

John W Perkins, 1935-2008 (Director, 1984-1994)

John Perkins exemplified the spirit of the University Department of Extra-Mural Studies of much of the second half of the twentieth century. John was a Devonian, as could be detected from his voice even after nearly forty years in South Wales. Despite strong south-western roots he chose Manchester as a university and studied geography there from 1953 to 1956. After that, he returned to Devon and by the later 1960s was working in adult education as a WEA tutor-organiser. Like a number of WEA tutors of the period, a move into university extra-mural work was a natural transition and he came to Cardiff early in 1971 to take up the new post of staff tutor in geology. He quickly expanded the geology programme and began the series of study tours for which he will be well know to many. These continued, even after he became Director of Extra-Mural Studies on the retirement of John Selwyn Davies in 1984, and took in all sorts of geological landscapes from Britain to the Pacific and from Iceland to the Grand Canyon. His period as Head of Department was not an easy one for Adult Education or for the university, but he ensured that the Department successfully weathered the storms and began moving it into the era when its courses were more closely aligned with those of the undergraduate programme. He took early retirement in 1994 on the onset of Parkinson's Disease. For many years, in retirement, he was able to control this debilitating disease, though latterly he was forced to resort to a wheelchair. He tried hard not to let this affect his independence or his mobility. Only a couple of months ago, I encountered him on a shopping expedition, assisted by one of his neighbours and cheerfully recounting his wheelchair adventures around various Cardiff venues.

John was a great believer in taking university knowledge into the community. Inevitably he did this through his courses, but he also was the author of a number of books which carried his subject to a much wider audience. His three volumes (on Devon and Dorset) in the 'Geology Explained' series are still quoted as standard handbooks for the area concerned. A number of books and booklets written by him were published by the University Department of Extra-Mural Studies. These were intended to provide a geological background for the layman on areas as diverse as the South Wales Coalfield and Arizona. He also published on the Bath Stone industry and on the stones of Cardiff – not in this case the underlying geology of the region but the often exotic stones used in the buildings of the Victorian and later city. All exemplified their author's enthusiasm for geology and his ability to convey both that enthusiasm and his considerable knowledge to a broad audience.

In the days before assessment of students came to dominate adult teaching, contacts between tutors and adult students were more easy-going and not necessarily restricted to a formal timetable. Certainly John regarded his students as his friends and many shared his love both of geology and of walking. One result was an informal walking society, termed by its members (most of whom were attending, or had attended, John's classes) the 'Hummocky Drifters' after a particular geological phenomenon often encountered in the Cardiff region. Its activities lasted long after John left the Department and eased both his retirement and, perhaps, the gap left by the early death of his second wife Ruth.

John once likened life to a bus journey with different people getting on and off at different points – a neat modernisation of Bede's analogy of the sparrow flying through the lighted hall. There will be many whose life will be diminished by the departure of this very particular traveller.' (PVW)

Gill Boden (Acting Director/ Director, 1994-1998)

John Perkins was obliged to retire prematurely due to ill-health in August 1994 and his departure heralded a particularly difficult period for the Department. The national accreditation framework had just been introduced and an accreditation scheme had yet to be developed at Cardiff in order to ensure eligibility for further Funding Council support for adult education courses. Consequently the Department was the subject of a review looking into its future. Indeed, consideration

The old infirmary building in Newport Road which
was the original home of the University College of
South Wales and Monmouthshire, 1883 & 1933

**Temporary science laboratories in
Newport Road, exterior and interior**

A G Little,
Professor of History 1892-1901

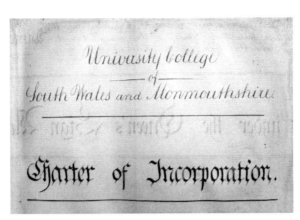

University College of South Wales
and Monmouthshire.

PROSPECTUS
OF

UNIVERSITY EXTENSION LECTURES

FOR THE SESSION,

OCTOBER, 1901, TO MARCH, 1902.

CARDIFF,
AT THE PRINTING WORKS.
1901.

**The University's Royal Charter
and prospectus for extension
lectures 1901-1902**

**Ronald Burrows,
Professor of Greek 1897-1908**

The University Settlement
buildings in Walker Road and
Courtenay Road

**Viriamu Jones,
Principal 1883-1901
A H Trow,
Principal 1918-1929**

**Ivor James,
Registrar 1883-1895
D J A Brown,
Registrar 1913-c1933**

**A F Dixon,
Professor of Anatomy 1897-1902**

Cardiff Centre for Lifelong Learning 2008

was being given towards following the path of other universities which had closed the doors of their extra-mural departments permanently. What could easily have been a catastrophe so far as adult education in Cardiff and its environs was concerned was averted by the concerted efforts of the staff within the Department who lobbied vigorously for its survival. A special tribute should be paid to Gill Boden, co-ordinating lecturer for social studies and psychology, who agreed to take on the directorship of the department temporarily (for about four to six months) at this very difficult juncture. Thus Gill, then the mother of two small children and a new-born baby, became the first female director of a department which was facing turbulent times. Indeed, her role as Director was confirmed by the Principal just days before a business plan was required before the University's review group. Due to a monumental effort by all concerned the business plan was successfully completed and accepted. Furthermore, 350 courses were finally accredited by Christmas of that year, an achievement made possible by the co-operation of part-time tutors, co-ordinating lecturers and support staff. Many 'adventures' lay ahead which saw Gill's initial agreement to act as temporary Director extended from four months to four years. Gill, who is retiring in 2008, has written a further reflective contribution in the final chapter of this study.

Madeleine Havard (Acting Director, 1998-2000)

Madeleine Havard joined the Department as biological sciences coordinator replacing Mary Gillam. A marine biologist by training, she gained her PhD at Cardiff researching marine worms in the Bristol Channel. Prior to her appointment in Cardiff, she had worked for the World Wildlife Fund and brought a good deal of management expertise to the Department. Acting as Assistant Director to Gill Boden during the mid-1990s, Madeleine took over as acting Director when Gill stepped down in 1998. Following John King's appointment as Director two years later, she, in effect, returned to her role as Assistant Director, a very necessary task given John's many other commitments. By 2000 it was clear that the University intended to look outside the Department for its new Dean of Lifelong

Learning and Madeleine took the, probably, easy decision to move back
into Nature Conservation as Chief Executive of the Wildlife Trust of
South and West Wales.

John King (Director, 2000-2002)

John King was an established head of section and professor when
he came to the Department as its head in 2000. Previously he had
run the Department of Maritime Studies which had been a victim of
reorganisations in the late 1990s. He also played an important part
in University affairs and was a pro-vice chancellor for much of the
period that he was also in charge of lifelong learning. It was John who
oversaw the move of the Department from Park Place to the building
in Senghennydd Road recently vacated by the Education Department
– the memory of which still lingers in room numbering within the
building. He also reorganised departmental administration and tackled
its recurrent financial problems. John's many University commitments
meant that his timetable was an extremely full one and his staff got
used to the sight of their head of department sprinting up or down
Park Place or Senghennydd Road and to the resultant rather breathless
starts to meetings. The Department undoubtedly benefited from
having a head who was close to the centre of university administration,
but the combination of departmental and university duties was not an
easy one for the university's most senior academics and were separated
by Dr David Grant soon after he took over as Vice-Chancellor. As
a result, John moved over to become the University's Director of
External Affairs and the new post of Dean of Lifelong Learning was
created.

Dr Richard Evans (Dean of Lifelong Learning, 2002 onwards)

Richard Evans was born and brought up in Wolverhampton, the
home of the finest football club in the country, at least in his
opinion! The reluctance to face facts, or at the least a tendency to
avoid them wherever awkward, led him naturally to the study of
ancient civilisations. This reached its high point in his doctoral research

on relations between the Greeks and the Persians, as illuminated by diplomatic practice from the ancient near east.

His parents were from North Wales and North-East England respectively so it made perfect sense to study in London, at University College. There he met his future wife, gained a degree and narrowly avoided a career in the Civil Service by gaining a research award – for 4 years! After that and while completing his doctorate – things were more leisurely in those days – he followed in his wife's footsteps and began teaching part-time for the University of London Extra-Mural Studies Department. This experience stood him in good stead when he applied for a full-time job with the equivalent department in Cambridge in 1981. Ten years later and after a variety of jobs within the Cambridge setup, he upped sticks to Manchester to run a consortium of universities' activities in high-level training and professional development. This led to supporting broader collaboration between universities in the regional HE Association, of which he was joint Director until 2002.

He counted himself lucky to have secured a return to the education of adults when appointed as Dean of Lifelong Learning at Cardiff University. The stimulation of having an immediate impact on real lives, whether those of colleagues or of adult learners, takes a lot of beating! Cardiff was there at the start of lifelong learning in universities back in 1883 and Richard plans for another 125 years of the leading Welsh university combining education of the highest quality with service to the local, national and global communities.

His media career has ranged from the *Petula Clark Show* on television and *Friday Night is Music Night* on Radio 2 to many concerts, broadcasts and recordings. In all cases he has played a tuba at the back of a brass band and if the conductors had had their way he'd have been outside in the car-park.

The Cardiff Centre for Lifelong Learning remains committed to its original aim of reaching out to those within and outside the city boundaries in order to bring opportunities for learning to everyone. Whether it is a vocational stepping-stone or a leisure-time pursuit for its own sake, the value of adult education can never be over-estimated. In the final chapter we will hear from some of the key members of staff who have ensured that the Centre for Lifelong Learning has endured and flourished over the past 30 years. We will then complete this study by looking to the future with a few words from the current Dean of Lifelong Learning at Cardiff, Dr Richard Evans.

Past, Present & Future...

Over the last 125 years, adult education in Cardiff has had to overcome a variety of hurdles, both large and small. The early years saw problems of funding and accommodation at a time when great demographic changes were occurring related to a slump in agriculture and phenomenal growth in industry. World War One placed pressure on all areas of life and, as we have seen, this included adult education. But despite leaky roofs, staffing shortages and significant funding deficiencies Cardiff's community engagement mission endured during these early years. The 1920s brought industrial unrest and a general strike, while the 1930s witnessed a world recession that resulted in hardship for many, culminating in the outbreak of World War Two. In the post-war era the University's adult education-community engagement provision has faced many new challenges and at times has struggled to survive. Yet, thanks to the collective efforts of the many dedicated and committed staff the Department has endured and flourished. The numerous courses (700 a year in almost 100 venues across South East Wales, including 25 'on-line' courses) currently run by the Cardiff Centre for Lifelong Learning embrace a diverse array of disciplines including Archaeology, Art & Architecture, Business & Management Studies, Computing, Creative Writing, Welsh (Cymraeg), Folklore, History, Languages, Law, Literature, Media & Photography, Music, Philosophy, Religion, Science and Social Studies.[115] Cardiff Centre for Lifelong Learning accredits courses at both first and second level undergraduate study. It has a turnaround of approximately 7000 part-time students with around 6000 of them undertaking assessment. This is equivalent to 430 full-time students, making it one of the University's largest departments. Indeed, the Centre represents a microcosm of the University as a whole; it is, if you like, the friendly and accessible face, or the 'shop front' of Cardiff University. Day schools and residential weekends, along with study trips in Britain and abroad remain popular and varied, and over a dozen short courses for professional development are also available.[116] A particularly exciting addition has been the establishment of the Confucius Institute in 2008. Under the guidance of the Ministry of Education in China and in collaboration with Xiamen University, the Institute, which is based at the Cardiff Centre of Lifelong Learning, offers courses in Chinese language and culture to members of the community, public and private sector organisations, as well as university staff and students.[117]

Yet, the final words on the Cardiff Centre for Lifelong Learning do not require the services of an historian. A number of co-ordinating lecturers who have given many years service to the cause of adult education have recently retired, or are about to do so, and they have generously agreed to share some of their experiences with us. What better way is there to draw this story to a close than in the words of some of the women and men who have been an integral part of the lifelong learning provision at Cardiff for the past thirty or so years?

Gwen Awbery, Welsh & Folklore

What sticks with you from the years with Extra Mural Studies; no – Continuing Education; no – Continuing Education and Professional Development; no – Lifelong Learning (apart from the need for new stationery)?

Good things. The students, who are there because they have chosen to come and want to be there. You can never predict what different experiences and insights they will bring to a class, and no two groups are the same. The tutors, who turn out in the cold and the rain, week in week out, and teach such an incredible range of courses. The freedom to experiment – to see if new subjects or new approaches will attract people, to see if running a course at a different time or in a different place will be a good idea. The challenge of setting up distance-learning courses, and being in close contact through email with students you never meet – students in north or west Wales, in Scotland, France, even the USA or Argentina. The times when you can see that a course has made a difference, and given someone the skills and confidence to go on and develop in a new direction.

Frustrating things. You set up a really good course with a very capable tutor, and then it fails because not enough people have signed on. Endless changes in the funding systems, as you try and minimise the disruption to ongoing classes and field furious complaints from students. Good ideas that fall through the cracks, because they don't fit the regulations in force at the time. The inevitable gaps in the help available for students with financial problems, so that people who really need the help and would benefit from the course have to pull out. The University's tendency to assume that all students are full-time undergraduates aged 18-21, and its consequent reluctance to provide facilities in the evening or on the weekend, or outside undergraduate semesters.

Compromises. Working out what you *can* do with the funding and resources that are available. Juggling timetables and locations to fit around tutors' other commitments, education centres' obligations to other providers, and trying desperately not to get stuck with a Monday class in the summer term which will hit up against all those awful bank holidays and go on forever, right into July when schools break up and everyone has other plans.

Never a dull moment. Definitely.

Gill Boden, Social Studies & Psychology

I joined the Department in 1977, coming from Reading where I had been teaching enthusiastic young trainee teachers. Returning to Wales to teach adults was daunting but exciting: the Department, in many ways, hardly resembled what we have now at all; my first impression was of an old fashioned gentleman's club firmly looking back to the nineteenth century and fittingly housed in two large Victorian 'semis' in Park Place. I was only the second woman staff tutor; the small administrative staff, known collectively as 'the girls' despite a mean age of 50, were referred to by their first names while we were called by our titles. This may not sound overridingly important but it made me very uncomfortable being expected to treat women twice my age in this kind of way: I'm glad to say that this and many other things have changed out of all recognition. We finally moved into the twentieth century at least.

One thing that has not changed, in my view, is that we offer to students a taste of the University. People are still impressed with the range and quality of what we have on offer and our part-time tutors continue to delight, dazzle and nurture our students. Our 'core business', despite accreditation, e-learning, continuing professional development and so on, has not fundamentally changed at all. We still exist for adults from all backgrounds to experience the joy of learning almost entirely for its own sake. When students leave us to continue at the 'big school' across the road or elsewhere we are pleased but we have no underlying agenda about where study should take our students so while I think that accreditation has been helpful to students and a good discipline for us as teachers, most of our students do not see our courses as a means to an end and so are highly motivated and a pleasure to be with.

Royston Havard, Music & Law

'Adult education is deliberately non-vocational in character. Its aim is to provide a liberal education for people who are already in various spheres of employment, and the whole organisation is founded upon the basic principle that the enlightenment of the public is socially desirable.' *Survey of Adult Education in Wales*, commissioned by the University of Wales in 1940

'In my most sanguine moments I find myself looking forward to the time when it will be considered necessary to have in every town and district educated teachers of the people as it is now to have pastors to look after their religious education.' R D Roberts (a key figure in the history of the University Extension Movement, who held important positions in the world of extension studies at Cambridge and London).

'When the University of Wales was being set up, there was, really, but one acceptable plan. The colleges were already in existence, and nothing was possible other than the incorporation of these into a University. And that is what was done. But some of Wales's foremost educationists had a very different form of University in mind… Its classes were to be held in every town and village throughout Wales. Its lectures and classes were to be held during workers' leisure hours.' Sir Owen M Edwards (who taught history at Oxford and, in 1907, became the first chief inspector of schools under the new Welsh Education Department). [Translated from the original Welsh.]

According to the *Report on Adult Education in Wales*, May 1970, commissioned by the Co-ordinating Committee for Adult Education in Wales, there were in Wales twice as many extramural classes in relation to population as in England. It was claimed – probably rightly – that this was largely the result of 'a system of voluntary religious education in the form of Sunday Schools for both children and adults of all ages, weeknight Bible classes and literary meetings'. One historian declared: 'on Sunday the whole country was turned into a school, where all taught and were taught in turn.' This tradition is obviously worth maintaining.

It seems to me that the sentiments expressed in each of the above quotations concerning liberal adult education are as appropriate and as relevant today as they were at the time of writing. They were my guiding principles while on the staff of the Aberystwyth and Cardiff departments, where most of my colleagues and I sought to provide the community with the opportunity to nurture its intellectual and cultural life, which was the original purpose of the adult education movement. Assessment criteria and academic measurement, which were introduced during the 1990s, have little to do with this. It is my fond hope that the wheel will soon come full circle, money being made available once again for this vital area of education.

I end by quoting two more persons who understood the purpose of adult education. Firstly, Sir Frederick Rees, Principal (1929-49) of what was then known as the University College of South Wales and Monmouthshire, in a broadcast on the Welsh Home Service in

April, 1953, on the occasion of the Workers' Educational Association's Jubilee: 'the maintenance of the democratic state depends on the disinterested pursuit of knowledge for its own sake and the mental discipline which free men learn in their search for it', and, speaking of Albert Mansbridge, founder of the WEA: '[it was] necessary to discard the conception of the educational ladder which a selected few could climb in favour of opening a broad highway which all could tread'; and, secondly, Goronwy Rees, Principal of the University College of Wales, Aberystwyth, during the 1950s, in the inaugural lecture at the Annual Conference of the University of Wales's Extramural Tutors held in Aberystwyth in July, 1954: '…in the work of our College there is no element which is more important or more essential than yours'. Goronwy Rees had already declared in his inaugural address as Principal in October, 1953: '…learning has its own virtues, of disinterestedness, of objectivity, of humility, and of integrity, and they seem to me to be the virtues of which the world stands in the greatest need today. It is precisely in so far as the universities have no utilitarian purpose, that they are the most useful of all institutions'.

John Pikoulis, Literature & Creative Writing

Teaching in the Centre from 1969 until 2006 resembled nothing so much as living in a state of permanent revolution. I don't doubt it will feel much the same to my successors. Everything changed, including our name and the way we were financed. On two occasions, we almost disappeared into the Education Department.

I was the first lecturer in literature to be appointed. At that time, I had only the sketchiest notion of 'extra-mural' but soon found how lucky I was. Teaching those who want to study and bring their own store of knowledge and experience with them meant that one learnt to talk to – not down to – them.

For many years, my programme constituted, in effect, an outreach of the English Department, but when that proved impossible to sustain, I relied instead on part-time tutors, gifted individuals who were outside the University but could contribute richly to it. Harnessing their talents is as important a function as any other the Centre serves. It also rooted our courses securely in the communities we work in.

Typically, we covered everything from Chaucer to contemporary literature. The programme included two annual schools, one on drama, the other on literature. (Glyn Jones's contribution to the latter was published as a Park Place Paper). There was also a lecture series based on A-level texts for schools and colleges as well as the general public. And, from 1990 on, there was the increasingly-popular and always enjoyable annual summer study tour.

The old Diploma in Extra-Mural Studies attracted younger (and often male) students but the accredited courses that followed proved less attractive and led to a drop in numbers. Even so, a flourishing literature programme is at the heart of any humanities provision.

As literature waned, creative writing bloomed. No such courses existed in 1969 and I have the melancholy distinction of introducing them to the University – 'melancholy' in the view of those who remain sceptical of its value as an academic discipline. Yet technical training in art forms – nobody, of course, can teach inspiration – is both an ancient and honourable activity. The fact that it reached literature late only reflects the changing circumstances of modern life. Again, I was lucky to be able to call on gifted individuals who carried higher education to places it had never reached before.

More craft-based courses followed when we accredited the courses run by the photography agency, Ffotogallery.

My teaching naturally went hand in hand with research, in particular into nineteenth and twentieth century British and American literature and Welsh writing in English. The books and articles that followed fed back to my classes and were, in turn, fed by them.

The sheer strength of the extra-mural tradition in Cardiff has had one contrary effect: the failure to develop degree studies, which I championed back in the 70s. Where other, and smaller, universities have gone, we have not followed. That points the way. And a research centre into our immediate hinterland, south-east Wales.

Peter Webster, Archaeology

Beyond the Pale: some thoughts on extra-mural life in the seventies:

The past, as we all know, is another country and never more so than when looking back over the best part of forty years. The Department which I joined in 1969 was a very different place from the one which I shall leave in 2009. It had recently moved into 38 and 40 Park Place, premises vacated by the BBC whose occupancy could still be detected – not only a functioning studio, but also an aerial still survived and was still used by the talking newspaper for the blind and a radio society. An even more enduring survival was a large building in the garden with a distinctly suspect asbestos roof. Those who knew about such things looked at it and muttered about structures designed for agricultural use. Those who lectured in this room in the dead of winter will long remember the inadequate nature of its outside door, which faced the prevailing wind, and the students still dressed in their overcoats.

So much then, for a past golden age. It did, however, have aspects on which one might these days stop and ponder. The Department which I joined had two tutors resident in the more far flung parts of the territory, whose job was to organise courses in those areas. It also had some seven full-time lecturers (then known as staff tutors), a Director and three administrative staff (the third was a recent addition). Courses cost about a shilling (5p) per lecture. Comparing costs across time is, as every historian knows, a tricky business, but it is undoubtedly true that, comparatively, the time spent on administration was far less and that spend with students far more. The earliest extant prospectuses reveal the staff tutor in archaeology running about the same number of winter courses as now, but he also ran a summer programme of site visits or fieldwork, and the 1970s also saw occasional summer schools outside Cardiff, day trips to a number of sites, and a number of tours (those to Hadrian's Wall and Rome stand out in the memory). The decade also saw a string of excavation and survey projects including the Cardiff Castle excavations from 1974 onwards and excavations elsewhere in the Cardiff area in many years. It may be that the energy of youth had something to do with this, but one cannot help but suspect that the student 'archaeological experience' has declined in proportion to the ever increasing 'accountability' of the 1980s and 1990s. There is no longer the time to write handbooks for foreign tours or organise some

60 people and their equipment onto a four-week excavation. Is it too fanciful to see another reflection of the same phenomenon in the ever-decreasing ratio of academic staff to administrative staff within the Department across those same decades (the 9:4 ratio of 1970 was 10:5 by 1979, but stands at about 11: 22 in 2008). Who has gained? One feels that it has not been the students – though we must also remember that, with the exception of those using Room 2.25 in the Senghennydd Road building first thing on a Monday morning in January, they also miss out on the necessity to wear their overcoats during lectures.

And in the 70s, it was all done without the aid of computers – how did we manage in those far off days?

Richard Evans, Dean of Lifelong Learning

I first taught an extra-mural class in 1978, as an hourly-paid tutor for the Department of Extra-Mural Studies at London University. I found it so stimulating and enjoyable that I leapt at the chance of a full-time job in the field when one came up at Cambridge University two years later. I have worked in extra-mural studies, continuing education (and training) and lifelong learning for nearly the whole of my career and have never (well, hardly ever) regretted my choice. It is a privilege to help people of all ages to find fulfilment through learning.

We can all be justifiably proud that Cardiff University's original charter includes the clear commitment to making knowledge accessible to as broad a community as possible. The underlying purpose – a well-educated and cohesive community – is as essential today as it was then. I would go further and argue that the increasing specialisation of higher-level learning means that individuals have in their initial education less chance to encounter knowledge of many kinds and to do so in the company of others. There is therefore even more need to provide access to these riches and – in addition – to make sure that people can interrogate cogently and use responsibly the information they encounter.

The story told in this small volume demonstrates how previous generations have responded to the challenge of pursuing knowledge of the highest distinction while at the same time serving the communities of which they were part. We can be sure that those who framed the original Charter of Cardiff University would have been versed in the debates of the day about the purpose of a university education, exemplified by this quote from Cardinal Newman:

> If, then, a practical end must be assigned to a university course, I say it is that of training good members of society. Its art is the art of social life and its end is fitness for the world.

Underneath this purpose, however, a university derives its identity from creating, conserving, sharing and applying knowledge. I conclude with the words of a modern exponent of that pursuit, David Starkey:

> The number of things we actually need to know to survive is very small. Most of the body of human knowledge is a glorious monument to redundancy. It's there because we want it to be there, because we take pleasure in it, because we're complex, difficult animals with a unique awareness of our environment which isn't just the physical thing; it is the whole environment of human experience accumulated and surviving.

Can we continue to combine the pursuit of knowledge with its application for the benefit of society, as those who framed the original charter intended? Yes, we can.

References

1   Expansion of technical/scientific education in Britain before industrialisation lagged when compared to Germany, whose school system developed ahead of industrialisation. As a consequence of the symbiotic relationship between university and industry, German products would, prior to World War One, flood the world's markets while, at the same time, 'its output of iron and steel outstripped even Great Britain's and was second only to that of the United States.' Cornwell, J (2004) *Hitler's Scientists: Science, War and the Devil's Pact,* Penguin, Harmondsworth, p. 43.

2   One of a number of non-conformist clerics at odds with church laws and customs. Despite being unpopular with some church dignitaries, the movement was a great success, and when Jones died in 1761, it was recorded that 3,495 schools has been established with over 158,000 scholars in twenty-five years. *Dictionary of Welsh Biography*. The National Library of Wales. http://yba.llgc.org.uk/en/index.html.

3   *Survey of Adult Education in Wales* (1940), University Extension Board, University of Wales, p. 7. Prepared by a Survey Committee acting on behalf of the Extension Board at the University of Wales. The Welsh Department of the Board of Education wished to identify the needs of adults in Wales and to determine the means by which particular needs could best be met, in order 'to implement such part of the Government's programme of educational reform as can be put into force without legislation.'

4   *Dictionary of Welsh Biography*. The National Library of Wales. http://yba.llgc.org.uk/en/index.html.

5   *Oxford Dictionary of National Biography.*

6   Harvey, A (1966) *One Hundred Years of Technical Education, 1866-1966*, Welsh College of Advanced Technology, Cardiff, p.12.

7   Harvey, A (1966) *One Hundred Years of Technical Education, 1866-1966*, Welsh College of Advanced Technology, Cardiff, pp 12-13.

8   Harvey, A (1966) *One Hundred Years of Technical Education, 1866-1966*, Welsh College of Advanced Technology, Cardiff, p. 14.

9   Harvey, A (1966) *One Hundred Years of Technical Education, 1866-*

1966, Welsh College of Advanced Technology, Cardiff, p. 12.

10   He was later to sculpt the statue of John Viriamu Jones which stands in the central hall of Main College.

11   Trow, A H & Brown, D J A (1933) *A Short History of the College 1883-1933*, Western Mail and Echo, Cardiff, p. 11.

12   Trow, A H & Brown, D J A (1933) *A Short History of the College 1883-1933*, Western Mail and Echo, Cardiff, p. 12.

13   A list of many of the names can be found in Cardiff Council Minutes for 1881-3. Cardiff Records (1905), Volume 5, pp. 62-84.

14   Trow, A H & Brown, D J A (1933) *A Short History of the College 1883-1933*, Western Mail and Echo, Cardiff, p. 12.

15   Elected August 18th – Lord Aberdare, Archdeacon Griffiths, Dean Vaughan, Dr W T Edwards (Cardiff), the Reverend J Cynddylan Jones, Principal Jayne (Lampeter), Principal T C Edwards (Aberystwyth), Professor Morgan (Carmarthen), the Reverend J D Watters, Mr F Sonley Johnstone, Principal W Edwards (Pontypool), and the Reverend Alfred Tilley. The Honorary Secretaries (who had voting power) were Mr Lewis Williams and Mr John Duncan. Six additional members were added three days later – ie, Mr Rudler, Professor Rhys, Mr Williams, HMIS, Mr Lascelles Carr, Bishop Hedley and the Reverend David Edwards of Newport.

16   Trow, A H & Brown, D J A (1933) *A Short History of the College 1883-1933*, Western Mail and Echo, Cardiff, p. 14.

17   Trow, A H & Brown, D J A (1933) *A Short History of the College 1883-1933*, Western Mail and Echo, Cardiff, p. 15.

18   The Anglican Church usually favoured the Tory party.

19   UCC R LB1 – Letter Book. 30/10/83 – 18/8/84, p. 749.

20   UCC Charter of Incorporation, 7th October 1884. This particular responsibility was reiterated on page one of Letter Book 2. UCC R LB2 Letter Book. 18/8/84 – 17/6/85, p. 1

21   Dr R D Roberts later helped to establish the University of Wales and was variously its junior deputy chancellor and chairman of its executive committee. He attempted, unsuccessfully, to get this particular clause included in the University of Wales Charter of 23rd November 1894. *Dictionary of Welsh Biography,* National Library of Wales.

22   Clifford, H & Davies, J Selwyn (1983) 'Department of Extra-Mural Studies' in Chrimes, S B (ed.) *University College Cardiff: A Centenary History 1883-1983,* privately published, p. 27.

23   Jones, G & Quinn, M (ed.) (1983) *Fountains of Praise, University College, Cardiff 1883-1983*, University College Cardiff Press, Cardiff, p. 75.

24 Harvey, A (1966) *One Hundred Years of Technical Education, 1866-1966*, Welsh College of Advanced Technology, Cardiff, p. 17.

25 *Oxford Dictionary of National Biography*. http://www.oxforddnb.com

26 *Oxford Dictionary of National Biography*. http://www.oxforddnb.com. Howard Spring's interesting life is captured movingly in his three autobiographical books: *Heaven Lies About Us*, *In the Meantime* and *Reminiscences and Other Things*. The three works were subsequently published in one volume: Spring, Howard (1972) *The Autobiography of Howard Spring*, Collins, London.

27 Letter Book 1 gives the figure as 150 day students and 625 evening students.

28 *Survey of Adult Education in Wales* (1940), University Extension Board, University of Wales, p. 15

29 UCC R LB2 Letter Book. 18/8/84 – 17/6/85, p. 341 (5/1/85)

30 UCC/R/LB2 Letter Book. 18/8/84 – 17/6/85, p. 50.

31 UCC/R/LB/2 Letter book. 18/8/84 – 17/6/85 p. 20.

32 Jones, G & Quinn, M (ed.) (1983) *Fountains of Praise, University College, Cardiff 1883-1983*, p. 13.

33 *Oxford Dictionary of National Biography*. http://www.oxforddnb.com.

34 *Cardiff Times*, 25th September 1875.

35 A pattern which can be observed in other newly established extension centres across England and Wales see Fieldhouse, R (1996) 'The Nineteenth Century' in Fieldhouse, R (ed.) *A History of Modern British Adult Education*, NIACE, Leicester, 1996, pp 10-46, 36-41.

36 *Survey of Adult Education in Wales* (1940), University Extension Board, University of Wales, p. 15

37 *Survey of Adult Education in Wales* (1940), University Extension Board, University of Wales, p. 15

38 *Survey of Adult Education in Wales* (1940), University Extension Board, University of Wales, p. 16

39 Clifford, H & Davies, J Selwyn (1983) 'Department of Extra-Mural Studies' in Chrimes, S B (ed.) *University College Cardiff: A Centenary History 1883-1983*, privately published, p.402.

40 Clifford, H & Davies, J Selwyn (1983) 'Department of Extra-Mural Studies' in Chrimes, S B (ed.) *University College Cardiff: A Centenary History 1883-1983*, privately published, p.402.

41 The Local Taxation Act of 1890 provided for the allocation of part of the income from duties on wines and spirits to help with this work.

42   Harvey, A (1966) *One Hundred Years of Technical Education, 1866-1966*, Welsh College of Advanced Technology, Cardiff, p. 15.

43   Harvey, A (1966) *One Hundred Years of Technical Education, 1866-1966*, Welsh College of Advanced Technology, Cardiff, p. 15/16.

44   Harvey, A (1966) *One Hundred Years of Technical Education, 1866-1966*, Welsh College of Advanced Technology, Cardiff, p. 16. (At the time this book was written, the Dumfries Place building was being used as a Students' Union by University College).

45   Born London 1842. Jewish by birth, he was at one time Professor of Mechanics at the Catholic University in London. An educationist and a leading authority on technical education in the United Kingdom, he was connected in an honorary capacity with many important educational institutions. He was also a member of the Royal Commission on Technical Education 1881-84.

46   Harvey, A (1966) *One Hundred Years of Technical Education, 1866-1966*, Welsh College of Advanced Technology, Cardiff, p. 17.

47   Harvey, A (1966) *One Hundred Years of Technical Education, 1866-1966*, Welsh College of Advanced Technology, Cardiff, p. 17.

48   Powicke, F M 'Little, Andrew George (1863–1945)' in the *Oxford Dictionary of National Biography.* http://www.oxforddnb.com/view/article/34556.

49   University Extension Lectures Minute Book, June 1901-2 UCC/Sn.CM/Ext. Lec./M/1. There was no evidence in this file of any of the responses.

50   University Extension Lectures Minute Book, June 1901-2 UCC/Sn.CM/Ext. Lec./M/1.

51   University Extension Lectures Minute Book, June 1901-2 UCC/Sn.CM/Ext. Lec./M/1.

52   Prospectus of University Extension Lectures, October 1901-March 1902.

53   In addition to the main Welsh towns mentioned above, the centres contacted included a very large number of smaller Welsh towns.

54   Full details can be found in Appendix I.

55   *Survey of Adult Education in Wales* (1940), University Extension Board, University of Wales, p. 17.

56   *Oxford Dictionary of National Biography.* http://www.oxforddnb.com/view/article/34556.

57   For a fuller study of the Settlement movements and their background see Fieldhouse, R (1996) 'The Nineteenth Century' in Fieldhouse, R (ed.) *A History of Modern British Adult Education,* NIACE, Leicester, p. 42-3.

58   Reason, W (1898) *Social Questions of Today: University and Social Settlements,* Methuen, London, p. 8.

59   Knapp, John M (ed.) (1895) *The Universities and the Social Problem: an Account of the University Settlements in East London*, Rivington, Percival & Co., London. Sir John Gorst (1835-1916) was a politician and lawyer. He served as Solicitor General for England and Wales from 1885-6 and as Vice-President of the Committee of the Council on Education between 1895 and 1902.

60   Rose, Jonathon (2001) *The Intellectual Life of the British Working Classes*, Yale University Press, New Haven, p. 256.

61   An enthusiast of the Greek people, their language and culture, he spent a lot of time in Greece. Ronald Burrows Street in Limassol was named in his honour.

62   Later Professor of Political Economy at Manchester. By the 1920s, Sir Sydney Chapman was Assistant Secretary of the Board of Trade.

63   Glasgow, G (1924) *Ronald Burrows, A Memoir, Nisbet & Co.,* London, p. 96.

64   Originally a house with a shop attached – shortly afterwards the shop next door was also taken over. Bull, B M (1965) *The University Settlement in Cardiff*, privately published, p. 7.

65   Glasgow, G (1924) *Ronald Burrows, A Memoir,* Nisbet & Co., London, p. 98.

66   Speech at the opening of the fourth session of the club on 23rd September 1904. Glasgow G. (1924) *Ronald Burrows, A Memoir,* Nisbet & Co, London, p. 98.

67   Professor Burrows also gave the opening lecture to the Workers' Educational Association at Barry (the first branch in Wales) in 1903 and in 1907 was instrumental in the establishment of the Cardiff Branch of the Association.

68   Bull, B M (1965) *The University Settlement in Cardiff*, privately published.

69   *Cap & Gown*, SCOLAR, Cardiff University. Box 1/102 1892-1903.

70   He accepted a chair in Greek at Manchester in 1908.

71   Bull, B M (1965) *The University Settlement in Cardiff*, privately published. GRO Acc. No. D/D CE 4/1-2.

72   It usually took two months or so for awards to be gazetted so he may well have won it at the third battle of Ypres at Passchendale.

73   Glamorgan Record Office D/D CES 1/13b.

74   Bull, B M (1965) *The University Settlement in Cardiff*, privately published, p. 18. GRO Acc. No. D/D CE 4/1-2.

75   Bull, B M (1965) *The University Settlement in Cardiff*, privately published, p. 18. GRO Acc. No. D/D CE 4/1-2.

76   Correspondence on University Settlement Buildings 1919. R/F/12.

77   Bull, B M (1965) *The University Settlement in Cardiff*, privately published, p. 19. GRO Acc. No. D/D CE 4/1-2.

78   The 1919 Report. The Final and Interim Reports of the Adult Education Committee of the Ministry of Reconstruction 1918-1919, The Making of the 1919 Report, p.27

79   Pate, W J (1972) *The History of the YMCA. in Wales 1852-1972*, The Welsh National Council of YMCAs, Cardiff, chapter 5.

80   The 1919 Report. The Final and Interim Reports of the Adult Education Committee of the Ministry of Reconstruction 1918-1919, The Final Report, p. 338.

81   These lines were transport/supply links running from base camp to front line (railways) and their static state often encouraged the growth of 'communities' along their length.

82   The 1919 Report. The Final and Interim Reports of the Adult Education Committee of the Ministry of Reconstruction 1918-1919, The Final Report, p. 338.

83   The 1919 Report. The Final and Interim Reports of the Adult Education Committee of the Ministry of Reconstruction 1918-1919, The Final Report, p. 343.

84   The 1919 Report. The Final and Interim Reports of the Adult Education Committee of the Ministry of Reconstruction 1918-1919, p. 9

85   *Survey of Adult Education in Wales* (1940), University Extension Board, University of Wales, p. 24

86   *Survey of Adult Education in Wales* (1940), University Extension Board, University of Wales, p. 23

87   Davies, J (2000) 'John Davies and the Workers' Educational Association in South Wales', *Llafur* 8 (1), 48-57, p. 52.

88   Two types of grant-earning courses were recognized by the Board of Education during this period: the three-year Tutorial Course and Pioneer Courses which served as a 'taster' which could, if its students proved to be both reliable and able, be developed into a Tutorial Course.

89   JCUT Classes Minute Book. UCC/CL.CM/JTCLCM/M/1.

90   Clifford, H & Davies, J Selwyn (1983) 'Department of Extra-Mural Studies' in Chrimes, S B (ed.) *University College Cardiff: A Centenary History 1883-1983*, privately published, p. 402.

91   The chief task of the secretary of the WEA at this time was to coordinate courses for the working classes, provided and financed by the

colleges of the University of Wales. However, many of the leading figures in Cardiff University were notoriously unenthusiastic about such a venture (a hostility shared by *The Western Mail*). The WEA was reliant to some extent on capitalist finance, for example the Davies family of Llandinam, chief shareholders in the Ocean Coal Company. Anxious to stave off criticism in this regard, its political radicalism during the General Strike of 1926 was emphasised, thereby divorcing it from Cardiff – education of radicals was not popular. However, this estrangement seems to have been short-lived. England, J (ed.) (2007) *Changing Lives: Workers' Education in Wales, 1907-2007*, Llafur, Cardiff, pp 30-31.

92   Guard Book (volume of invitations, posters & programmes to lectures and concerts 1913-1925) UCC/MICS/G/2.

93   Guard Book (Volume of invitations, posters & programmes to lectures and concerts 1913-1925). UCC/MICS/G/2.

94   Influential on social policy in Britain, a key figure in the establishment of Toc H and an influential figure in boys' club work, he is perhaps best remembered as a prison reformer. The basic idea underpinning his approach was that the primary aim of detention was to educate the offender towards rehabilitation. Smith, M.K. (2004) 'Alexander (Alec) Paterson, youth work and prison reform', *the encyclopedia of informal education,* www.infed. org/thinkers/paterson.htm.

95   Pate, W J (1972) *The History of the YMCA. in Wales 1852-1972*, The Welsh National Council of YMCAs, Cardiff, p. 54.

96   Coincidentally, Professor Foxley was one of the university lecturers who had volunteered her services during the war (see Appendix 2) but there is no indication as to whether her students were of civil or military origin. Minutes of the Joint Committee for University Tutorial Classes, October 1917. UCC/CL.CM/JTCLM/M/1 & 2.

97   Also in 1930, a sum of money (£100) was allocated so that an extra-mural section could be established in the library of the University College for use by all extra-mural students.

98   Trow, A H & Brown, D J A (1933) *A Short History of the College 1883-1933*, Western Mail and Echo, Cardiff, p. 78.

99   Clifford, H & Davies, J Selwyn (1983) 'Department of Extra-Mural Studies' in Chrimes, S B (ed.) *University College Cardiff: A Centenary History 1883-1983,* privately published, p. 402.

100   Clifford, H & Davies, J Selwyn (1983) 'Department of Extra-Mural Studies' in Chrimes, S B (ed.) *University College Cardiff: A Centenary History 1883-1983,* privately published, p. 403.

101   Clifford, H & Davies, J Selwyn (1983) 'Department of Extra-Mural

Studies' in Chrimes, S B (ed.) *University College Cardiff: A Centenary History 1883-1983,* p. 403.

102   Clifford, H & Davies, J Selwyn (1983) 'Department of Extra-Mural Studies' in Chrimes, S B (ed.) *University College Cardiff: A Centenary History 1883-1983,* privately published, p. 403. The possibility of appointing a Director of Extra-Mural Studies for the Cardiff and Swansea areas jointly was also suggested but, despite much discussion, this did not happen.

103   See Clifford, H & Davies, J Selwyn (1983) 'Department of Extra-Mural Studies' in Chrimes, S B (ed.) *University College Cardiff: A Centenary History 1883-1983,* privately published.

104   Clifford, H & Davies, J Selwyn (1983) 'Department of Extra-Mural Studies' in Chrimes, S B (ed.) *University College Cardiff: A Centenary History 1883-1983,* privately published, p. 404.

105   Clifford, H & Davies, J Selwyn (1983) 'Department of Extra-Mural Studies' in Chrimes, S B (ed.) *University College Cardiff: A Centenary History 1883-1983,* privately published, p. 404.

106 Courtesy of   Dr Peter Webster, Reader in Archaeology and Coordinating Lecturer in Archaeology and the Ancient World and Art and Architecture, Cardiff Centre for Lifelong Learning, Cardiff.

107   Clifford, H & Davies, J Selwyn (1983) 'Department of Extra-Mural Studies' in Chrimes, S B (ed.) *University College Cardiff: A Centenary History 1883-1983,* privately published, p. 403.

108   Clifford, H & Davies, J Selwyn (1983) 'Department of Extra-Mural Studies' in Chrimes, S B (ed.) *University College Cardiff: A Centenary History 1883-1983,* privately published, p. 403.

109   Royston Havard, Cardiff Centre for Lifelong Learning – personal communication.

110   These instrumentalists included: Denis Matthews, Agustin Anievas, Charles Rosen, Julius Katchen, Gerald Moore, Ingrid Haebler, John Lill, Craig Sheppard, Shura Cherkassky, Christopher Hogwood, Peter Hurford. Royston Havard – personal communication.

111   http://www.cardiff.ac.uk/music/newsandevents/events/concerts/07hodges.html .

112   Sir Donald Wolfitt was an English actor/manager who was knighted in 1957 for services to the theatre – in particular his Shakespearean roles. Lord Birkett was a barrister and judge who presided at the Nuremberg War Criminal Trials as an alternative British judge. He became Lord Justice of Appeal.

113   Clifford, H & Davies, J Selwyn (1983) 'Department of Extra-Mural

Studies' in Chrimes, S B (ed.) *University College Cardiff: A Centenary History 1883-1983,* privately published, p. 404.

114 Clifford, H & Davies, J Selwyn (1983) 'Department of Extra-Mural Studies' in Chrimes, S B (ed.) *University College Cardiff: A Centenary History 1883-1983,* privately published, p. 405.

115 Build-up of points from accredited courses can lead to a Foundation Certificate (60 credits at Level 1 within one subject area), Certificate of Higher Education (120 at Level 1 with any combination of courses), or a Diploma of Education (120 at Level 2 in pre-defined 60-credit study blocks).

116 Full details of all courses and classes can be found on the Cardiff University Website – http://www.cardiff.ac.uk/learn/.

117 Full details of the Institute can be found at http://www.cardiff.ac.uk/learn/confuciusinstitute/.

Appendix I

Prospectus 1901-02:

Lecturer	Title of Lecture	Classes
W. S. Boulton, Geology, UCC	The Geology of the South Wales Coal Field	5 or 10
H. Bruce History & Eng. Lang. UCC	Landmarks of English Literature Some Aspects of Welsh History	4 or 6 4 or 6
R. M. Burrows, Greek, UCC	The Greek Tragedy The Greek Comedy Homer and the Homeric Problem Introductory Lectures on Greek Art A Journey in Greece	4 or 8 4 4 or 8 10 4
A. G. Little, History, UCC	Mediæval Wales Social Life & Institutions in the Middle Ages	5 or 6 5 or 6
H. Littledale Eng. Lang. & Lit. UCC	The Lake Poets (Wordsworth, Coleridge, Southey)	6
J. S. Mackenzie, Philosophy, UCC	Elements of Social Philosophy	6
J. P. Maine Exhibitioner	Folk-lore – the Science of Fairy Tales with special reference to the tradition	

Jesus College Oxford	of Wales	8
J. H. Morgan Brakenbury Scholar Balliol, Oxford	Feudalism in England and Wales, its economic, legal, and governmental aspects The Hundred Years War with France British Colonies and their Constitutions South African History, and the Constitutional History of the Boer States	4 4 4 4
T. Rees, Theology, Memorial College, Brecon	Some Economic Problems (Labour, Poverty & Wealth)	8
W. G. Savage	Bacteriology and its Practical Applications: i. A general account of bacteria and their position in nature; ii. Bacteria in air, water and soil; iii. Fermentation and allied processes; iv. Microbes in food, especially milk and meat; v. and vi. Bacteria and Disease.	6
S. Vincent Histology, UCC	Popular Physiology	8 or 10

Appendix I (cont...)

Prospectus 1902-03:

Lecturer	Title of Lecture	Classes
W. S. Boulton, Geology, UCC	The Geology of the South Wales Coal Field	5 or 10
	The Scenery and Geology of South Wales	5 or 10
	The Geological History of the British Islands	5 or 10
H. Bruce History, UCC	The Renaissance	6
	Four Great English Poets (Chaucer, Spenser, Milton, Keats)	4
R. M. Burrows Greek, UCC	Greek Tragedy	4 or 8
	Greek Comedy	4
	Homer and the Homeric Problem	4 or 8
	Introductory Lectures on Greek Art	10
	A Journey in Greece	4
Miss A. M. Cooke History, UCC	The Viking Age	6
	Monastic England	6
	Great English Churchmen (Anselm, Langron, Wiclif, Wolsey, Wesley, Newman)	6
	The History of Wales	6
J. G. Davies, Headmaster Neath County School	Four Great Men (Julius Caesar, Oliver Cromwell, Napoleon Buonaparte, Bismark)	4
	Some National Heroes (Julius Caesar, Buonaparte, Nelson, Bismark)	4

E. H. Davies Builth County School	The Development of Scenery	6
A. F. Dixon Anatomy, UCC	The Organs of the Senses (Sight, Hearing, Taste and Smell; the Skin as a Sense Organ; Comparisons of the Various Sense Organs	6
P. G. Gundry Physics, UCC	Light and Colour The Electric Current and its Application	6 6
C. J. Hamilton Political Science, UCC	Social Movements of the Nineteenth Century Labour Questions of the Day The Duties of Citizenship Ruskin as Social Reformer The Problem of the Distribution of Wealth	4-6 4-6 4-6 5 4-6
A. H. Hope Greek & Latin, UCC	Rome (Statesmen, Men of Letters, Economy and Private Life – end of Republic, beginning of Principate) Some Great English Novelists (Fielding, Richardson, Austen, Scott, Dickens, Thackeray, Eliot, The Brontës, Mallock, Meredith)	6 5
Ivor B. John English & French, UCC	Mediæval Romance Tennyson and his relation to 19th C. poetry Matthew Arnold as Poet and Critic The Mabinogion – their Mythology and Romance	6 5 6 5-10
J. Morgan Jones Aberdare	The Protestant Reformation The Age of Milton	6 8
J. S. Mackenzie Philosophy,	The Elements of Ethics The 'Republic' of Plato	10 10

UCC

J. P. Maine Jesus College, Oxford	Folk-lore – the Science of Fairy Tales, with special reference to the traditions of Wales	6 or 8
	Early Civilization; development of language, writing, arts of life, early religious beliefs, etc.	6 or 8
J. H. Morgan Balliol College Oxford	The History of the late South African Republics	tba
T. Raymont Education, UCC	Principles and Practice of Teaching (intended chiefly for teachers)	6
Thos. Rees Memorial College Brecon	Some Economic Problems (Labour, Poverty, Theology, Wealth)	8
Miss Joan B. Reynolds Geography, Oxford	The History of Exploration	6-10
W. G. Savage Bacteriology, UCC	Bacteriology and its Practical Applications: i. A general account of bacteria and their position in nature; ii. Bacteria in air, water and soil; iii. Fermentation and allied processes; iv. Microbes in food, especiallymilk and meat; v. and vi. Bacteria and disease. The Principles of Hygiene: i. Air and Health; ii. Water and Health; iii. Food and Health; iv. Soil and Health;	6 or 8

Occupations and Disease;
v and vi. Infectious Diseases – their
propagation and relation to sanitation.   6

Some single (pioneer) lectures were also offered, ie:

Milton, Bunyan, Cromwell, Ruskin; Alfred the Great; King Arthur
Stories; Sketches of Mediæval Times; The Beautiful in Modern Poetry;
The Earliest Page of Celtic History; Life in a Mediæval Monastery;
Giraldus Cambrensis; The Debt Modern Civilisation Owes to Greece;
Athens; Tales told by our Ancestors; Coronation.

Appendix II

Lecturers giving their services free to deliver a special course of lectures
(taken from minutes of the Joint Committee for University Tutorial Classes,
October 1917).

Professor Foxley

1.   The general situation of education with respect to actual teaching
        (single)
2.   Rousseau's *Emile* (5 or 6)

J. H. Shaxby

1.   Historical Sketch of Foreign Policy (single)

Mr J. G. Smith

1.   Co-operation in Agricultural Production
2.   Co-operation in Agricultural Distribution
3.   Science and Agriculture
        (These illustrated by reference to the work of the I.A.O.S. and
        Irish Board of Agriculture).
4.   The Problem of the Unskilled Labourer in Rural Districts
        (also offers help on courses in Economic Theory or History of
        Revolutionary and Social Movements).

Mr Hedger Wallace

1.   Colonial Temperate Agriculture
2.   Colonial Tropical Agriculture
3.   Indian Agriculture
4.   Factors of Agricultural Production

5.   Guiding Principles in the Organisation of the Farm
6.   Production of Fertilizers (2)
        (a) Basic Slag and Superphosphate
        (b) Nitrate of Soda, Sulphate of Ammonia and Potash
7.   Commercial Products from Milk.

Select bibliography

Archival sources:

Cardiff University

Correspondence on University Settlement Buildings 1919. R/F/12.
Guard Book (volume of invitations, posters & programmes to lectures and concert: 1913-1925). UCCIMICS/G/2.
JCUT Classes Minute Book. UCC/CL.CM/JTCLCMIM/l.
Minutes of the Joint Committee for University Tutorial Classes, October 1917. UCC/CL.CM/JTCLM/MI & 2.
Prospectus of University Extension Lectures, October 1901-March 1902. RLB 1 – Letter Book. 30/10/83-18/8/84.
UCC Charter of Incorporation. 7th October 1894. UCC RLB2 Letter Book. 18/8/84-17/6/85.
University Extension Lectures Minute Book June 1901-2 UCC/Sn.CM/Ext. Lec./M/1.
Cap and Gown (May, 1905) New Series, No 5.

Glamorgan Record Office

Glamorgan Record Office D/D CES 1/13b

Published sources:

Bull, B M (1965) *The University Settlement in Cardiff*, privately published.
Chrimes, S B (ed.) *University College Cardiff: A Centenary History 1883-1983,* privately published.

England, J (ed.) (2007) *Changing Lives: Workers' Education in Wales, 1907-2007*, Llafur, Cardiff.

Fieldhouse, R (ed.) *A History of Modern British Adult Education*, NIACE, Leicester.

Glasgow, G (1924) *Ronald Burrows, A Memoir,* Nisbet & Co., London.

Harvey, A (1966) *One Hundred Years of Technical Education, 1866-1966*, Welsh College of Advanced Technology, Cardiff.

Jones, G & Quinn, M (ed.) (1983) *Fountains of Praise, University College, Cardiff 1883-1983*, University College Cardiff Press, Cardiff.

Knapp, John M (ed.) (1895) *The Universities and the Social Problem: an Account of the University Settlements in East London*, Rivington, Percival & Co., London

Pate, W J (1972) *The History of the YMCA. in Wales 1852-1972*, The Welsh National Council of YMCAs, Cardiff.

Rose, Jonathon (2001) *The Intellectual Life of the British Working Classes*, Yale University Press, New Haven.

Spring, Howard (1972) *The Autobiography of Howard Spring*, Collins, London.

Survey of Adult Education in Wales (1940), University Extension Board, University of Wales.

Trow, A H & Brown, D J A (1933) *A Short History of the College 1883-1933*, Western Mail and Echo, Cardiff.

Index of names

Cardiff Centre for Lifelong Learning
Canolfan Caerdydd ar gyfer Addysg Gydol Oes

www.cardiff.ac.uk/learn
www.caerdydd.ac.uk/dysgu

Check our website for details of courses currently available at the Centre.